HOLD ON SIS, LET ME TAKE MY WIG OFF!

By Staci Purpose Kirk
As told To
Nicole D. Miller

The Memoir of A Warrior

Hold On Sis, Let Me Take My Wig Off!
The Memoir of A Warrior

By Staci PurPose Kirk
As Told To Nicole D. Miller
Copyright © 2024

All rights reserved. This book or any thereof may not be reproduced in any manner whatsoever without the express written permission of the publisher except for the use of brief quotations used for the purposes of a book review.

Foreword by Dr. Shamarah J. Hutchins

It is an absolute honor to introduce my dear friend and accountability partner, Staci PurPose Kirk, whose story has touched my heart in ways I cannot fully express. Staci is more than just a six-time cancer survivor; she is the embodiment of resilience, faith, and a deep-rooted strength that transcends adversity. In this remarkable memoir, Hold on Sis, Let Me Take My Wig Off, she opens her heart to us, sharing the unfiltered truth of her journey with a vulnerability that is both raw and inspiring.

I have had the privilege of walking alongside Staci, witnessing her unwavering commitment to not only surviving but thriving in the face of unimaginable odds. Her strength isn't just in her ability to fight but in her unyielding faith and the hope she carries for herself and others. Through every trial, she has remained a lighthouse for those around her, and this book is her gift to women everywhere—a reminder that even in the darkest moments, there is always a flicker of light waiting to guide us through.

Staci's words are a lifeline for anyone facing their own battles, and her journey reminds us that we are never truly alone in our struggles. Her story is not just one of survival but one of triumph, one that will strike a chord deeply with women from all walks of life. It is a call to embrace our own inner strength, to dig deep into moments of uncertainty, and to have faith in the miracles that are yet to come.

To know Staci is to witness the living proof of what happens when faith meets an indomitable spirit. In her, I see not only a survivor but a leader, a warrior, and a friend whose story will undoubtedly inspire generations of women. I am endlessly grateful for her presence in my life and for the privilege to share in this journey.

Sis, as you take off your wig, may every woman who reads this book feel empowered to shed their own layers, to stand boldly in their truth, and to believe that no matter the storm, they too can rise.

With love and admiration,
Dr. Shamarah J. Hutchins
TheMindologist

A Reflection From 2019

Sitting in my office, it's 11:26 pm. I'm tired. My body continuously feels as if a Mack Truck has run over it, backed up and repeated the assault. Still, I know there is work to do. That is the story of my life and has been the story of many women's lives generation after generation. So, here I sit. Candle burning, condensation forming on my wine glass while cookies (that are not allowed on my new 2019 diet) stare at me as if to say, "Come on. Just eat me! There is no sense in fighting it."

You see, truly this is the year of my reset button. At 45 years old, I've decided, no scratch that, I have been propelled into my true self. It took unforeseen circumstances and uncomfortable situations to force me into becoming who I always was... who God intended me to be.

All this time I had been practicing. Gearing up for the big stage. Rehearsing entrepreneurship, practicing motivation and inspiration; a PurPose in training. Boy, over the years I exuded confidence. My stride was head high, shoulders straight and purposeful. Looking in from the outside, most people assumed I had it all together. Don't get me wrong, sis, according to the average American's standards, I did have it all together. I had a 'good job' where I was tolerated in management because they had no choice but to acknowledge my intelligence and keen business savvy. I was married with two kids and a dog. We owned our home with two cars. I dressed nice, my kids were awesome... so I was doing great, right?

Wrong. I, like many other women who would care to admit it, was bent and contorted on the inside. Every single day my soul teetered on the very edge of breaking. In the silence of my struggle, I worked harder, over-achieved at everything I could get my hands on and became a master of whatever I put my mind to. I did all this because if I sat still longer than 30 seconds, I would have to deal with being sexually abused as a child, molested by family, married to an addict and emotional abuser, divorced, afflicted by several assaults of cancer, being the hated black female executive, and all the things that came along with being ME.

I honestly can't tell you if I was born with a high tolerance for emotional pain (as I think women in general are) or if God gave me supernatural abilities when needed to overcome things before, they ever happened. It sounds crazy but as you read these stories of my life, you will start to see that despite the gory details regarding these events, I somehow managed to make the effects of trauma ricochet off me. When confronted by friends and associates demanding to know why I wasn't balled up in a corner somewhere in the fetal position, I simply replied, "For what? I'm good. I'm sure worse things have happened to other people." It was only later that I would find out that the sum of my experiences could only be found in a room full of different people with their experiences combined. Even writing this now, I find it hard to believe that I've really had it any worse than anyone else.

What I do know for certain, though, is that not enough people share their experiences. Most run from trauma and negative events so they would never even consider bringing them up to others. However, this is where I like to define the meaning of survivorship. Our experiences make us who we are, but they have a far more important role within our existence. We were created to be a help to others. When we survive something, it is our duty to ensure that someone else benefits from that survival. Sharing the tools of our own storms that led to personal triumphs and breakthroughs, is what connects us to our greater purpose. That's my heart with this book. That you would glean from the resilience I had to manifest to overcome the various obstacles that kept coming at me. And if I could do it, know that you can do it too.

"No matter what she's going through, her PurPose is to inspire and motivate, her voice is powerful from motivational speaking to thought-provoking poetry. Her words have moved me in many ways."
- Charlie Ezell Jr.

CHAPTER 1: RAINBOWS & SKITTLES

God dressed me in long legs, knock knees and boobs for days. My lanky form was often mistaken for the substitute teacher when I entered the classroom. I swear I've been the same height since second grade and haven't grown an inch since! I even dwarfed my principal when he congratulated me while handing me an award in sixth grade. It's like God armed me for adulthood, and my physical form was a foreshadowing of the adult experiences that would occur because my childhood was actually more like an adulthood, making me the quintessential outsider. This was made even more prevalent when we moved from East Cleveland to Cleveland Heights, Ohio.

Cleveland Heights High School was a culture shock. I was used to the down-to-earth, rugged style of 'EC', as we still call it to this day, which vanished with the move. If you're not from Cleveland, let me tell you these two residential areas couldn't be more different. Think about the popular movie from 1988, School Daze. I had clearly been in the world of 'jiggaboos' (which I loved in the movie and in life) to a brand-new world of 'wannabees'. Now don't get me wrong, I was well liked and tended to make friends easily, but I never really fit in. I was an old soul swimming in the world of beat faces, flashy name brands, and runway fashion. Oddly enough, in my old 'hood, I was considered the "bougie friend". I was well taken care of financially, and all my friends knew that when they came over to spend the night, they'd get the princess treatment! The thing is, the stuff my Cleveland Heights peers were so concerned with, trendy apparel and aesthetics, diminished in comparison to what was on my mind. I truly had an adult mind stuck in an adult body attached to a child's age. I was bored with the daily conversation of shallow gossip and cliques. I had always had such a larger view of life, even then.

Born an only child to my mother, I was often the latch-key kid. When your mom is the only working parent in the household, forever juggling two or three jobs, it can be that way. But I didn't complain. That is until my father decided to put his hands on me. That was the beginning of when what little childhood I had got snatched. That was the beginning of when I would know for certain that I was different.

The thing is, kids only know something's wrong when someone else tells them something's wrong, so when the molestation started, I really didn't have a clue that it was an issue. I had swallowed my father's lies, even the one that insinuated that my mother was 'the other woman.' And you can't tell the main woman she's less important than the other woman, even when she is just a ten-year old child and even when the man is her father.

My grandmother got ahold of this news and told my mother. My mother questioned my father and me about it, but he sat there on the living room couch and gurgled his lies. I was shocked. I'm sitting there, on the floor in front of them both, wondering, why aren't you telling her about us? As if he was my man denying our very valid relationship. In my mind, we were in this thing together. That's how twisted he had my thinking; he was a true master manipulator. And it wasn't just him using me himself, but he passed me off to his brother visiting from Alabama. "Just rub some lotion on his back," my father told an 8-year-old me, and things elevated from there.

You may not understand this, but for some reason, I had the ability to not even be mad at my dad. He came from the south in Alabama, where incest and molestation seemed to be the norm. At least back then. My father had 12 other kids besides me, and one of my sisters came up pregnant with a little girl who we believe to be his child. Someone found a love letter between them. Sadly, I wasn't the only one he had done this too.

So, I had all that going on by the age of 14 when cysts appeared under my underarms. The cysts were the result of Follicular Lymphoma, but we didn't know that then. In fact, I didn't know that until my second bout with cancer at age 23. But at 14, I was having these outbursts with these gigantic cysts under my arms, and let me just say, when they burst, the odor was no joke. Now you know, if you can smell you, then everybody else can. If there is one thing any teenager does not want in school, it is an odor. Your peers will roast the mess out of you. I wasn't about that roasting life, so anytime I had an outburst, and I knew that odor was soon to follow, I left and cut school. It's better to miss school than to be somebody's verbal punching bag. Thankfully, I was able to dodge the typical school bullying that often accompanied puberty. My large size was a definite asset when it came to folks trying to punk me. Maybe God spared me in that way because I was going through so much on the home front. That cyst odor situation lasted about two months until my mom found me a dermatologist. One thing I'll say about that woman is that even though she was carrying the financial load and working her butt off, she was quick to react when I was in need. All I had to say was a word, and she searched for a solution.

When we went to the dermatologist, the doctor suggested that they remove my sweat glands. The issue was that they didn't do any other research as to what caused the cysts. No biopsies. No testing. Not even a follow-up appointment. They just removed my sweat glands in surgery, inserted 27 stitches on one side of me and 24 stitches on the other, and called it a day. That by itself is an indication of the medical system we're dealing with in this country and the racial injustice plaguing it. This inaccurate archaic belief that Black men and women are inhuman and can endure unfathomable amounts of pain ranges from the abuse of participants of the Tuskegee study to the stealing of Henrietta Lacks's cells. Sadly, centuries have gone by, and minorities are still being neglected and mistreated by the medical industry.

As a child, I wouldn't have been privy to all of that, though. It's only after boxing three different types of cancer in six different rounds that I can see how let down I've been by a slew of medical professionals. And I know I'm not the only one. I have no doubt that if someone had just done their job back then, the excessive circumstances I endured in battling cancer would have been diminished. But I'm a glass-is-half-full kind of girl with a "rainbow and skittles" mentality, which I no doubt inherited from my dear mother and adopted later in life from my best friend. As a result, all I can say is that since I went through all that I did, I guess it was to help someone else.

My innate positive outlook, coupled with a mentality of being "God's soldier," helped me push through a lot. Even the molestation wasn't something I was going to let define or stunt me, though it did open the door to recurring sexual abuse. When you're a little girl in a woman's body, I guess it's a given to have to keep fighting unwanted male attention. In some ways, my body felt like a curse, and I was simply never comfortable in it. I didn't ask for boobs in the third grade and would have handed them over to the next passersby. I didn't ask for my older male cousins to view me as anything other than a little cousin. That happened too often simply because my mother was a workaholic and couldn't monitor me the way a traditional mom could. I was the only child of her generation, so I ended up playing with her first cousins, who were all boys and all older. My mom being MIA gave ample opportunity for my dad to take advantage, too. Being at home with a womanizer and molester day in and day out, there's bound to be abuse. But I refused to let negativity be my overall view of these situations. Instead, I used my setbacks to equip myself to be a life guide for others. I created recipes of success and healing to share with my clients in my life coaching business. I set out to make my mark on the world, triumphing over the many setbacks that kept being launched my way. With every hardship and difficulty, I fought for joy. I would rather laugh than cry any day, and I think that was why I went through cancer so many times because I was the type to overcome any obstacle.

"God only gives the hardest things to His toughest soldiers", was the saying back in the day. So, in order to be a good soldier, I shouldered up, stuck out my chest, and endured. Even when it meant almost losing my life.

Little woman child wears her robe inside
As summer drifts by
On cool Lake Erie winds
Playin' house in a home that transforms into hell
Like the heat of the sun outside
From nine to five
If only she could be outside

Little woman child wears her robe inside
When the children knock on suspecting doors
She is closed off to games that adulthood
Doesn't allow you to play
No, she can't come outside today

Little woman child adorned in lies
Told by those who were meant to protect her
Escapes the playground as it grabs at her grown woman-size
Long legs and thick thighs
Standing in knee socks and a big bird t-shirt

Her eyes don't water for you
Her mind doesn't become lost for you
Her body doesn't break for you
Her heart doesn't stop beating for you
Her faith doesn't waiver for you

Little woman child all grown up now
Holds her head higher than ever before
Knowing her path had to cross yours
To fulfill a greater purpose
So, don't worry wherever you are...

That little woman child,
Forgives you.

> *"Being around PurPose is like witnessing the embodiment of strength and selflessness. Even in her toughest battles, she radiates resilience and compassion, always prioritizing others' success and well-being over her own. To know her is to love her. Being in her presence, you can't help but to be inspired."*
>
> *- Taya Belle*

CHAPTER 2: THE ELEPHANT IN THE ROOM

"Your dad's been touching you," my aunt looked at me and said.

My eyes grew big, and I ducked my head, suddenly fascinated by the crisp cream carpet. How did she know? How could she tell? Was I wearing a sign? The only safe place I had back then was my grandmother and the woman we all knew as her best friend who lived with her. I called this woman my aunt. The truth was that my "aunt" was actually my grandmother's lover. But I didn't care what she was. To me, she was my hero. She was the flyest thing around and definitely the "femme" of the two. Even still, when it was time to throw down, she was ready, always carrying a loaded weapon. My aunt also had what some would call "the gift" and could perceive something so many around me seemed to be missing. She could perceive I was being molested.

"Please don't tell!" I begged, peering at her with fearful eyes. I was terrified for people to know. I loved my dad. I didn't want him to get into trouble. But my aunt wouldn't have demonstrated her love for me if she kept this ugly secret to herself, so she told my grandmother.

My grandmother was an "OG" in every sense of the word. She was a ball of fire and no joke. You did not want to mess with her. One time she got robbed and tried to fight the robbers! They were like, "Lady, sit down somewhere, or we gone' have to tie you up." You see, these were nice robbers, and they really weren't trying to hurt an old lady, but they underestimated this woman. Do you know they ended up having to tie her up to keep her off of them? That's the woman who found out about my molestation, so you can imagine her response. She went banging on my mom's front door, screaming to be let in. That's how my mom found out. My grandmother was raging, screaming accusations and demanding I be taken from that house and live with her. But my mother is the stark opposite of my grandmother. If my grandmother is a blazing fire, my mother is the calm sea. She assured my grandmother she would handle it, and her way of handling it meant asking my father and believing his lies.

I know that people are going to be upset with me because I wasn't upset with her. But when you're a victim of abuse, your psyche concerning it is different from those who haven't suffered in that way. My mother, too, was a victim of abuse. When she was a child, and her parents divorced after only ten months of marriage, her grandfather was awarded custody. He didn't want her growing up "in that lifestyle" with my grandmother and her female partner. Ironically, he's the one who became the culprit for my mother's traumatic childhood, which ensued after he married a woman who used him for money and beat my mother daily.

One time, right after Thanksgiving, my mother asked for leftover turkey, and her stepmother pulled out the remaining turkey, sat it on the floor, and made her eat the whole thing! My grandfather watched and did nothing. Even at 73 years old, my mother still has flashbacks of her abuse. As her daughter, I saw her as a delicate flower, and I often played the role of tending to and caring for her. Her past is what led her into my father's arms, and most in her family considered her the black sheep because of it. Her family was a bit uppity and frowned upon her marrying this 'Backwoods Bama,' so we kept our distance from them as a result. For some reason, even with their disapproval, she held onto my father even tighter. Maybe she wanted to show her family the two of them could make it. Her grip on him certainly wasn't because my father was this big financial contributor. She was the one working all the jobs and paying all the bills. He was as lazy as they came. She really didn't get much out of the relationship, as he didn't offer her true love or romance. It was a sad situation. My father simply loved being a kept man.

My grandmother was a bulldog, though, so even though no consequences came from my dad's actions, there was safety in knowing the truth had been revealed, and all I had to do was say the word, and she would rescue me. But I never did say that word. As is typical of victims of abuse, I struggled with the feeling that somehow, this thing that happened was caused by me. I often wrestled with the question, *Am I to blame?* Added to that feeling was the complicated experience of my abuser being my parent, and there was this misguided allegiance there. I was the main woman, so how could I leave him? I'm the one to care for my mother. I'm her emotional rock. I'm her protector.

How could I leave her? So, I'm bound to these two people who are now tiptoeing around the elephant in the room. We all had our various ways of coping. My mother became the "yes" parent. That meant anything I wanted, I got. All parental rules and boundaries flew out the window. I pretty much did what I wanted when I wanted. Thankfully, I was a good kid, so I didn't abuse my power too much. But still, imagine the message her way of functioning was sending me. I am a child with adult privileges. I make adult decisions over my life. I have adult responsibilities. Then there is my father, who I no longer see as my father. I never had a real father. I had a man who never saw me as a child and only viewed me as a woman. His woman. My way of coping with that trauma was poetry. Poetry became my outlet for the horrific events in my household.

I loved poetry because it was the escape from the tough, ugly mess of my reality. I could craft a tunnel of words on a page to unleash what I was never allowed to speak out loud. With poetry, I could create the world I wanted, needed and deserved. One where there was protection and justice. One that didn't permit the cruel experiences of my body being exploited early and often. Poetry was my therapy. I was so into writing that I became a published author in the third grade and was recognized in a huge school program at Kirk Junior High. Academia is where I shined. I was drawn to African

American literature and mythology. Even though I hardly studied, I still loved learning. Learning came easy and is one of the few traits I received from my father that was a benefit. He was lazy because he was so intelligent. He would start and stop school often because he was so much smarter than who was teaching him and what he was learning. I had that same conundrum. I never went to college because I never needed to.

In school I was looked at as a sort of child prodigy. I attended a magnet school which is a school with a specialized curriculum for advanced students. I was the go-to student for teachers and principals, and they had me in a case study held by Case Western Reserve University, where I was pitted against a student who wasn't as bright. My gift of intellect and my passion for poetry were the ways of escaping from the harshness of my circumstances.

I was also involved in the school choir and loved music. Additionally, I had a teacher who was pushing entrepreneurship, which was super rare back then. I was able to learn how to be a boss at a young age, both in my personal experiences and in her academic training. In my personal life outside of school, my grandmother and aunt were frequent outlets.

I thrived in their presence and fed off the electrifying energy of their lives. They were always throwing card parties, running numbers, and having a good time. Though the apartment they lived in was on the east side of Cleveland in the inner city, and there were mice and all types of things surrounding the unit, their place was immaculate! There was the cream carpet that you better NOT spill anything on, old antique furniture, and set-in-gold-trimmed high-back chairs. Our cups were always overflowing with juice (although my aunt's cup had something other than juice), sitting on matching glass tables. The sweet sounds of Jeopardy frequently crackled in the background on the TV screen. It was a palace in my childhood eyes, and they were the queens. Money was often flowing in plain sight at their parties, and I adopted the toughness they both demonstrated that my mother lacked. They were straight-up gangsters! Today, we would call them female bosses.

I had friends around back then, too, but I received a huge letdown when these very friends didn't believe me after I confided in them about the molestation. It hurt to finally have the courage to voice what was going on and have the very people I had been there for scoff in disbelief. Trust was definitely broken and was something I struggled to build with others after that. Being violated will stunt your ability to trust, and then having the people who are supposed to have your back turn their back and look the other way solidifies that experience. As much as I felt let down by my mother, I could give her grace because even at a young age, I understood her own dysfunction. But these friends didn't have her issues. Their unbelief caused me to question myself. How could they not believe me? Does that mean I made this whole thing up? It took me a while to see their perception. My father came off as "that dude." He was fun, funny, good-looking, and charismatic. He was the one that everyone felt good around. How could there possibly be a monster lurking underneath? He was a genius when it came to deflecting with humor. I inherited that trait as well.

One friend in particular did see through. It was a hot summer day, and she came to my door to ask me to come out and play. I appeared in my terry cloth robe and told her I couldn't and that I had to stay in the house. The look in her eyes said it all. She knew. My father stopped the molestation soon after that. He realized others were starting to know, and it scared him, but the damage had been done. My childhood was officially nonexistent. I was a fully blown adult. And maybe that was what was needed for me to combat cancer the way that I have. When you're fighting demons in your own house, the one in your body is just another one added to the collection. When your own father tries to take you out, everything else is going to pale in comparison.

"When I think of PurPose the first word that comes to mind is Resilience ...and the second is Service. It's amazing how after all she's been through, she still takes the time to honor others. A great human and Light."
- Marissa Jackson

CHAPTER 3: STILL I RISE

My mom was and always has been my best friend. From the beginning, it has been me and her against the world. Even when said world consisted of a narcissistic, manipulative womanizer who took up too much space in a house that didn't belong to him. Our home was a side-by-side-duplex, and I know for a fact that I wasn't the only one going through it. I could hear my next-door neighbor getting beat to death on a regular basis. Those walls were so thin; she probably heard what was happening to me, too, in the middle of the day when my mother was working.

It seemed my father's molestation was connected to that duplex we lived in in East Cleveland. During my time living in that home, I was haunted by nightmares and night terrors every single night, but I never told anyone. It wasn't until I was older that I shared this experience with my mother, and guess what? She was having nightmares in that house, too! Once we talked, we were able to fit the pieces together.

My mother told me that one night, my father had a visit from his deceased mother. Now, I was raised by a good-old Christian, faith-based mother, and when it comes to mysticism, some of these things are frowned upon in religion, but when reality becomes evidence, it can't be denied.

"Where's my granddaughter?" My father's mother said that when she visited him, I could just imagine him trembling when he told her where my room was! And this is where my mom's piece fits with mine. After that night, I told my mother, "Jesus visited me last night!" and I described in detail the big ball of white light that appeared over my bed. "It feels like a weight has lifted!" I proclaimed. That was my first experience, and I remember feeling safe and my personal relationship with God deepening. I started trusting God to protect me. Before then, I was so afraid to let God in.

I attended church regularly with my mother up until that point, but my father was always sowing negative seeds in me about it. "You go 'head go down in that water, and you ain't never gone' be the same!" he would taunt about the act of baptism. For a long time, I was so afraid to be baptized as a result of him instilling this fear in me. But once I had that spiritual encounter with my grandmother, I was free. I finally felt secure, and I was no longer fearful of his threats. That's when my view of my father started changing. I started lashing out at him. "There's nothing you can do to me!" I would sneer. He was despicable in my eyes. He was worthless, and I became downright disrespectful, letting him know exactly how I felt. "Don't talk to me!" I would tell him and go on about my business. That's when I had to start processing losing a dad. I released this in poetry and by writing letters. I wrote about the expectations I had of having a good father and how those expectations were snuffed out. Every child needs a dad, and daughters and sons need them in different ways. As a daughter, I would need a father to teach me the importance of knowing my worth and setting the standard for interested men who wanted to be with me. Because my foundation was shattered through his violation, my choices in men would be skewed.

But I didn't know all of that back then. Like many, I had to learn by going through it.

My early teen years were the time when I would experience the typical exploration of relationships with the opposite sex, though I wasn't yet open to sex. More than likely, this was due to my history of abuse, but also, it was probably because I was a super responsible kid. I started volunteering at a hospital around this time. That volunteer position would eventually turn into an actual job.

I had one close friend at the time who was as loose as they came. She would give anything to anybody and was super in touch with her sexuality. At 14, my head was focused more on building a life that I could be proud of and one that would pave the way to success. I was working and learning. I was thriving in accomplishments and achievements. So, when another instance of sexual abuse occurred, it was a shock. I hadn't given any signal that I wanted it. I had said "No" a hundred times. But the young man who raped me denied this, saying I wanted it. Saying I asked for it. Isn't that the typical response of abusers? They know good and well you didn't want it, but in order to cope with their demonic acts, they try to put the blame on you. I agreed that I had invited him over to watch a movie, but even with that invitation, I made it clear that he wasn't getting anything. I explicitly told him that we were just going to hang out. I even suggested that if he wanted sex, he should hit up my loose friend, who was giving it away like government cheese. He assured me on the phone that that's not what he was after. He flipped the switch really quickly, though, when he came over, and I discovered the true monster that he was. "My dad's gonna kill you!" I screamed when it was over, and he hurried to leave, saying, "No! You wanted it!" He even called me afterward, threatening me on the phone not to tell. Telling me I wanted it. But he knew I didn't. Even years later, when I saw him, he hurried to look the other way, pretending as if he didn't recognize me. He knows what he did was wrong.

Now, remember, this was the same year I was dealing with those cysts. It seemed my little life was bombarded with trauma and pain as I attempted to push forward and attain greatness. Those cysts were just the beginning of what I would face with the affliction of cancer in my body. They were a preview of what was to come. They were also a picture of how uniquely I was wired. There are very few on this planet who have dealt with the monstrous levels of abuse and trauma on so many fronts that I have. Similarly, the type of cancer I would experience was rare for an African American female to contract. Hodgkin's Lymphoma shows up in white males. How in the world did a young Black female become its target? How in the world did I become susceptible to so much so early? It is the mystery of God. All I knew back then was to keep moving forward.

"Bad things happen." "What happens in this house stays in this house." "Oh, that happened to you? That happened to me, too." These were the mantras and beliefs of the day and the ones I adopted. I wore them as badges of honor on my "good soldier's" uniform. That meant I kept a lot to myself. I didn't feel safe in relationships and friendships. My friendships were often one-sided. You can tell me all about your business, but I'm keeping my cards close. Even when my friends finally did come around and believe me about my father's abuse, it was too late. I had my guard up.

My mother was a constant picture of the tolerance of abuse. She bent over backwards, trying to give me the world to make up for not kicking my father out. If she admitted he was wrong, then she would have to do something about it. She was too afraid to do anything about it, so she buried her head in work and lavished me with gifts.

Because we didn't talk about our issues back then, there were no tools like counseling to process them. My process was to write and to hold onto a deeper sense of purpose. I actually found that being sick as an adult caused me to work even harder. Being faced with insurmountable obstacles and brutal affliction transformed me into a phoenix. The phoenix is a mythical immortal bird who becomes born again by rising from the ashes of its predecessors. I was a phoenix who would rise and triumph over and over again. But just as I would be fighting to survive in my home as a child, I would be fighting in my marriage as an adult. Unbeknownst to me, I would marry a man who housed the exact negative characteristics of my father. And it would take 24 years for me to spread my phoenix wings and fly away.

"When someone asks me about Staci ("PurPose"), it's hard for me to find adequate words; strength, courage, loving, helpful, etc. Stacy has a positive aura that surrounds her and everyone in her presence. It is a rare privilege to meet someone that special."

- Bonnie

CHAPTER 4: YELLOW WITH POLKA DOTS

Being a teenager in the 1980s was a special time. We had a skinned Michael Jackson, the unrivaled birth of hip-hop, jerry-curl-dripping style, and roller-skating fun. By then, I had hit my stride with men and made sure to keep me a cutie, whipping a nice ride that took me everywhere I wanted to go. Landing a man was never an issue, even with all the history of sexual abuse I had going on. One of the gifts victims of abuse have is the ability to compartmentalize. It is truly a protective mechanism to cope with the horrors of reality. By the age of 16, my new reality was flexing my teenage body that had been parked on the lot since grade school but was now finally ready to test drive. In the midst of me having a good old time in my personal life I was working hard. The same way I kept myself a man, I kept a job. But sometimes the craziness of my household bled into my work life.

One day, while working at a convenience store off Noble Rd., in walks my father. Apparently, he owed the manager some money because she had given him some items in good faith. When she asked him about payment, he mumbled something about getting her his money while easing out the door. I was so embarrassed. I shook my head and handed over my paycheck to pay his debt. That was the stuff my father was notorious for. He was constantly insulting my mother, verbally abusive, and cheating. One time, I actually caught him in the act, rolling around in bed with another woman. Sadly, my mother put up with all of it. She is a naturally bubbly person, greeting him every morning with kindness and a sweet countenance. "Good morning!" she would chirp. My father would ignore her as if she hadn't said a thing. She would ask, "What's wrong?" and he would be quick to say, "You." His tongue was a sharp sword that could cut down a giant into two feet. I cringed every time I witnessed their interactions, but this was my mother's choice. What could I do?

She allowed him to keep her car whenever she was at work while he would be off somewhere drunk, doing God knows what in it, which made him late picking her up. She endured his criticism about a house he hadn't dropped one lick of sweat to buy. He was a freeloader in every sense of the word, and it seemed the only thing my mother got out of the relationship was having someone to care for. She needed to be needed as much as he needed to use someone.

My father was also a drama queen. On any given day, he would fall out on the floor in the middle of the kitchen and pretend like he had passed out. My mother would freak out, scurry to his side, and fawn all over him. But I could see straight through his facade. "Mom, let's call 9-1-1," I would cross my arms over my chest and calmly suggest. Sure, as I suspected, my dad would pop up as if nothing had happened. It was all for attention. Tell me, then, why I could see so clearly through my father's shenanigans and yet be utterly blinded by a man with the same issues.

It was the beginning of summer, right before my senior year when I got swept off my feet. So much so that I traded the flashy Mazdas and Trailblazers of my dates for a man with a legit hoopty. We met at my friend's boo's house, where I had caught the bus to get to. Never in my teenage life had I caught a bus to meet a man. Never had I swapped the nice ride for the nice bike. And that's exactly what my ex-husband was rolling on when we met. A two-wheel, 10-speed, handlebar-having *bicycle*. I should have known then. On top of that, he wasn't paying me at all the attention I deserved for having made that crazy commute to see him! Here I am in the backyard of my friend's boo's house at the picnic table, going out of my way to make this thing happen, and he's acting like his good looks have trumped the need for him to be gushing all over me. *Please.* But somehow, we hit it off, and in no time, I was under his spell. His combined fineness with swag was the black magic trick that did me in. So much so that you couldn't tell me his rusty yellow station wagon wasn't a sparkling new Cadillac! That thing had so many rust spots I called them polka dots. My mother saw him pull up in it to pick me up one day, and the look of confusion on her face was comical. *Where is the Mazda?* I know that's what she was thinking! But he was my very first love. He was the first guy I stayed out all night with. I was the good girl, and that simply did not happen. Well, until him. I could have ridden off into the sunset perched on the handlebars of his 10-speed, two-wheeler. That man turned my water on!

I don't think your first love is anything anyone is completely ready for. The bubble gut butterflies. The high of being with that person. The addictive obsessive thoughts of needing to be with them when you're apart. I had all of that. I would have followed my first love to Kalamazoo! I honestly believe someone should put a warning label on young love, bottle it up, and toss it into the ocean. We are simply not to be trusted with all that Oxytocin shooting all over the place in our little bodies. You're bound to be foolish while drunk on all those hormones and chemicals. And foolish I was. I gave him the cookies and at 17, ended up pregnant. The thing is, I wasn't really that upset about the pregnancy. I had always been adamant about being a single mom due to a deep-seated fear that my children would endure the sexual abuse I had. I felt the safest way to protect them was to raise them alone. So, when I gave my baby daddy, at the time, the news and he tried to bolt, I shrugged. Fine. I'll do this myself.

Isn't that the worldwide Black woman's anthem? Technically I had been raised in a two-parent home, yet still saw my mother doing it all. The message I received in my home was that a man's responsibility was minimal if not nonexistent. Maybe that's why when my boyfriend figured out he was actually going to stick around and help me with this child, I took him back. I really didn't expect much and excused his waywardness as a result. The thing about my then-boyfriend was that his mother treated him like crap. When he all of a sudden proclaimed he had given up pork, the woman cooked pork every night. When that happened, he started eating with me and my mom. "Come on, we are going to Red Lobster!" my mom would proclaim, and the three of us would jump in the car.

We had some good times during its early stages, but our relationship would soon be tested. My pregnancy resulted in hyperemesis gravidarum. That meant there was no end to severe, intractable vomiting and nausea throughout the pregnancy. I became bedridden. I dropped 60 lbs quickly and looked like a bonafide crack addict. I couldn't keep anything down. I would be rushed to the hospital to receive fluids through IVs only to leave and be back again. My mom was a rock and would take me to all of my appointments. She and I would make attempts to even go out to eat. When I saw something scrumptious on TV, my mouth would water, and my eyes would light up. "Mom, let's go to Red Lobster!" I would suggest. I was so gung-ho when we got there, but after one piece of shrimp, it was over. I couldn't keep it down.

At this point, I was still living at my mom's house, but I refused to be a baby momma. I wanted a wedding before my child was born. We went through the whole shebang for a backyard wedding. I had the food, I had the decorations, I had the pastor, but do you know what I didn't have? A groom. Once again, he bolted, and we didn't get married at that time. Here I am, going through hell, risking my life to carry this man's child, and he doesn't even have the guts to marry me. I should have left then, but the truth is I was just as toxic as him. He was in a gang. He had been in and out of jail. He was a bad boy through and through. Additionally, he started demonstrating signs of mental health issues. He even managed to lose the station wagon once he got arrested, and it was impounded! All this, and I looked the other way, telling myself I could change him. I think, on some level, I wanted what I didn't have. A strong, safe family to raise my child in.

School was its own thing because Heights High didn't even give me the option to attend because I was pregnant. They kindly assigned me a tutor and informed me I would be learning at home. Do you know I saw that tutor one time and one time only? The whole time of his visit, he acted as if my having a teenage pregnancy was a communicable disease. I ended up taking the GED and calling it a day.
So I'm out of school, unable to work most days, and going through hell physically. Though my pregnancy nearly took me out, I pushed through. It was crazy, too, because even though I was losing so much weight, my baby was gaining weight. *Is he eating* my insides to stay alive? *I* wondered, only slightly kidding. Still, my body wasn't able to produce milk because of my malnutrition and deficiencies. All of this did not stop my tenacity to have this child, though. It wasn't until the doctor alluded to me not being able to carry full term and the possibility of having to take my baby early by C-section, that I became alarmed. I was determined to have my son vaginally and not early!

On top of the excessive nausea, I was allergic to the nausea medication. I soon learned I was just going to have to work through the nausea. There would be no easy way around it. Every time I took it, my body would react in convulsions. One time, my body even bent backward and got stuck in position! While at the hospital, the medical staff would turn me around to weigh me so that I wouldn't see the rapidly declining numbers on the scale. The social workers were constantly checking in with me. They were afraid for my sanity and didn't think I was in my right mind because I was determined to keep this child, regardless of how much the pregnancy was diminishing my body and my health. What they didn't know is that I was built for this. I was built for an onslaught of mental, emotional, and physical suffering. God had made me for it. And because of that mindset, I endured.

"My mother is the best and brightest person I know. Throughout every struggle and hardship she's faced, she's remained optimistic and full of hope. In her position, with her stories, others would not have been able to get to where she is today. They would have given up faith and let their hearts harden to the world long ago. Instead, she has devoted herself to serving her community and building others up. She is a hero to many and to me most of all."
- Jasmyne (her daughter)

"My experience with her as she fights this fight is that she is the definition of a strong woman. I've seen the weakness in her eyes, but I've also witnessed the strongest in her heart. She refuses to let anything beat her, and at the same time, she can smile like an angel. Queens are born and very rarely made."
~Mike Craig

CHAPTER 5: SUDDEN DEATH

At age 23, one day, I noticed this huge lump on the right side of my neck that felt warm. I worked at a medical professional's office at the time and figured I could get some answers there. I was wrong. They told me it was nothing and sent me on my way. It took six different doctors just to get the correct diagnosis. Six doctors until I was finally diagnosed with Hodgkin's Lymphoma. Initially, I was told it was Mono or some other minor infection. Part of the issue was that the lump caused discomfort and was painful to the touch due to inflammation. Cancer is not normally painful (but the treatment is), so I think that was throwing people off. The other issue is that Black people are often viewed by the medical profession as inhuman, which stems from our history as slaves when we were treated as property. It took two whole biopsies for the doctors to take me seriously. It took my determination to not allow the false reports to be my final report. I was frustrated, in pain, and weary. All of that was unnecessary heartache caused by a system that, to this day, looks the other way when Black men and women cry for help. The Hippocratic Oath states that doctors should "Do by their patients as they would be done by." The intention behind that statement is for medical professionals to do everything possible to save the lives of their patients the very way they would want their own lives saved. Five doctors before my final doctor buried this oath beneath a series of pat answers and uncaring attitudes. I could have died had I accepted their diagnosis, and my blood would have been on their hands.

I long for the day to see the scales balanced where men and women of color are valued enough for the Hippocratic oath to be upheld by all health professionals, not just a handful. I long for the day when we don't have to fight for just treatment in addition to fighting a life-threatening illness in our bodies. I pray for the day when we can walk into a hospital, say that something is wrong, and be believed - when we no longer have to prove our case through an invisible legal system while our health is deteriorating every second of that process.

After finally finding the right doctor, she took the extra step to do a needle biopsy right there in her office. I had this horrible fear of needles, and to make matters worse, the needle for the biopsy that was used was huge. I knew that something was wrong, but I didn't know what, and so my nerves were on ten, but I had finally found someone who was taking me seriously, so I was willing to do what it took. This was the first time someone had listened in the six months of me trying to get answers. It was the first time my voice was heard, but it was just the beginning of this uphill process.
The next biopsy was a new level of pain. It felt like someone had surgically removed my head from my neck and then screwed it back on. A bone marrow biopsy was also done, which is a staging test to ensure there was no metastasis to the bones. It was grueling. To qualify for chemo, I had to do a PET scan (Positron Emission Tomography), where minerals were put into my blood, and the blood flow was observed through radioactive imaging. There was the MUGA scan used to monitor my heart since the medication I would be taking could cause heart damage. There were various breathing tests until I was finally ready (physically per the tests) to start chemo. Every two weeks, I received a cocktail of four different drugs that caused me to be sick for 12 days. On the 13th day, I'd be better, only to receive more chemo on the 14th day. I did six cycles of chemo every two weeks for four months and watched the 4a strands of my hair drift to the floor. With chemo, everyone wants to talk about the hair loss, but no one wants to talk about the tooth

decay. Let me tell you, losing your teeth is a big deal, too. And even if you don't actually lose them, they're loosening inside of your mouth, threatening to flee at any second. For good reason, I am now deathly afraid of the dentist.

In the midst of this, I'm getting my blood drawn constantly. When you have cancer, there is always someone taking your blood. Over and over they were taking my blood, and, lucky me, I have something called nonexistent veins. That means it's really hard to find my veins, so I got poked more than the typical person. At one point, a nurse drew my blood without gloves on. I'm thinking, Why does this woman not have gloves on? Silly me, I trusted her as a professional and let her do her job. Well, guess what happened? My tests showed that I contracted Meningitis. That meant I had to have a spinal tap done. They proceeded to stick me seven different times for this spinal tap. Then the spinal fluid leaked, which caused spinal headaches to where I couldn't even move. Imagine a migraine on steroids. That's how bad those headaches were. And because they couldn't perform the spinal tap correctly initially, they kept sticking me.

The medical staff did all that, and I didn't even have Meningitis. It was a false report because this woman decided to take my blood without gloves on. I then had to get a blood patch where they injected blood into my back to patch the holes. They also had to put me under a fluoroscopy to get fluid. At that point, I was done! I wanted to leave. I wanted to quit. I wanted to give up. Hodgkins isn't that bad, I was thinking. But I didn't. I jumped through all the painful hoops, trying to get to my healing.

By the time I got diagnosed, my baby's father and I had been married for four years as he finally put a ring on it after standing me up the first time. Unfortunately, my marriage was a roller coaster speeding downhill fast, and the monster my ex-husband truly was quickly being unmasked. I was constantly being put down verbally and abused emotionally. "I always get second best," he would tell me. "I never get the prom queen." When I would refute his statements, he would try to turn it around. "That has more to do with me than you." As if that made it okay to tell me I'm someone's second choice. He was a master manipulator and loved to play mind games. I came home one day to him sitting with a gun to his head as if he was going to shoot himself. I freaked out and fawned all over him, but it was all a ploy. I was acting the same way over him that my mother had, with my father fainting on the kitchen floor. It's sad to say that the similarities did not end there.

My ex-husband was in the Navy when I got diagnosed. He had enrolled after losing his job, so the Navy became our main source of income. He was stationed on base and was approved for leave to come home to Cleveland to be with me. His superiors did everything they could to get him stationed downtown so he could help me during this process. Do you know I didn't see that man once while I was going through chemo? He was out every night, seeing women and doing drugs. The one time he came around during my treatment, he ranted about the medical bills he claimed he was paying for. Not once was he concerned about my well-being and what I was going through. My mother sat there by my hospital bed, seething. To make matters worse, he never even paid those bills. My mother helped get them written off by hospital management. That was when my eyes started to open, and I realized the narcissist that he was. That's when I started pulling away emotionally. But it would get worse before it got better.
I think part of the reason it took me so long to leave him was that I didn't have an expectation of being treated well since I never saw this between my parents, nor did I receive good treatment myself from my own father. Half the time, my father didn't even know what grade I was in. He had no interest in me as his daughter whatsoever. He ran around on my mother, got into drugs, and mistreated her relentlessly, even living with another woman at one point while carrying on an affair. My mother was so fragile that I had to be the strong one. I was so used to being the rock for my family since I had been playing that role since childhood. Even when I was diagnosed with Hodgkins, and the doctor informed us that a side effect of chemo was "sudden death," I had to be the rock. I peered at my ex-husband and mother, who looked as if their dog had just died. "It's okay. It's all going to be okay," was my immediate

response. Here I am, facing "sudden death," and I'm comforting them! But when you're raised in a home to be the rock, it's hard to turn that off. It's hard to lean on someone else, especially when there's no one else to lean on. So, when I was in the thick of it in my marriage, I took the abuse. I took the pain. I internalized it all. I shouldered it like a good soldier.

Even when I went through my second pregnancy and the trauma and hardship escalated, I kept it moving. I was carrying twin boys, and the hyperemesis gravidarum was in full effect. The problem was that now I had not just one but two growing fetuses in my body. My body was simply not going to survive the pregnancy. Even still, I did not want to hear it. I was determined to have those boys, but by week four I was almost dead. I had lost so much weight and was so malnourished that the pregnancy was literally killing me. Everything I went through with my son was now doubled. That's when the doctor put his foot down. "You're not going to survive these twins," he said with a grim expression. I called my ex-husband. "They won't let me have them! I can't do this!" I cried. I was heartbroken. I couldn't see giving up my children, even with all the pain they were causing. The doctor said that one twin's heartbeat was slower than the others, and in my mind, that meant they had a chance to live. The doctor even had the nerve to show me the fetuses in the ultrasound. What mother is going to be able to end her children's lives seeing their little bodies on an ultrasound? Somehow, some way, I was going to capitalize on that slim chance for my babies to live.

The doctor even had the nerve to show me the fetuses in the ultrasound. What mother is going to be able to end her children's lives seeing their little bodies on an ultrasound? Somehow, some way, I was going to capitalize on that slim chance for my babies to live. My ex-husband responded that I needed to terminate the pregnancy with a D&C. It was the only way I would live; he rationalized. Though he was able to help me come to that realization, he didn't come to the hospital and be there for me in person. Once again, he was MIA. Once again, I was on my own. And though it hurt, I was used to it.

"From the 1st day I met PurPose I knew she was a special kind with a bright light that had much to give & share with the world. She is too kind even to those who mean her NO GOOD but the person she is doesn't allow her to see the bad, hate, or evil in people all she sees is the greatness they can be or possess and makes it her business to help them see & be it as well no matter sick she is or what she may be dealing with herself. The best way I can put it is she can't have a selfish bone in her body!! She is one of the strongest women I know!"
- Lynn Chaney

"PurPose showed me what true faith is. Just in the time of me knowing her, she has battled cancer at least twice and every time she has never shown fear, doubt, or discouragement. She just kept on living as if that wasn't the scariest thing to have to go through. She continues enjoying life and advocating for everybody who has/is going through the same battles that she has faced numerous times. For these few reasons alone I work towards having the type of faith that she has."

- Key

CHAPTER 6: AN INNOCENT BYSTANDER

I can look back now and see that I was repeating my mother's dysfunction by choosing my ex-husband for a spouse. I was drawn to him because I needed to be needed, just as she needed to be needed by my father. I saw my ex as a project and someone I could make better. Like many, I had to go through it to learn that someone like that is bound to take you under with them. You can't save a drowning man who doesn't want to be saved, and truly, that man was drowning.

Though my ex had shown signs of mental health issues throughout our relationship, it wasn't until he was officially diagnosed with bipolar disorder that I finally had proof of his excessive mood swings and irrational behaviors. The sad thing is instead of getting on prescription medication and utilizing the health insurance options he received through the Navy; he became heavily dependent on drugs and alcohol, which led to an addiction. As you can imagine, our relationship was as turbulent as waves crashing during a storm. His verbal and emotional abuse was on ten, and I was called every insult in the book, from fat to stupid to ugly. This, of course, escalated to physical abuse. I once made the mistake of touching his arm while asking him a question, and he swung without hesitation, giving me a huge black eye. Throughout all of this, he was cheating across the globe wherever he was deployed. Dealing with a cheating, abusive, addicted narcissist with untreated bipolar disorder causes its own set of traumas, yet I had Hodgins' Lymphoma, a child to care for, and the aftermath of losing my twin boys to contend with. I wish I could say there was a break at home after losing those boys, but as soon as I returned from the hospital, I was faced with more drama. My grandmother lived downstairs in our four-unit apartment and was watching my son while I was in the hospital getting the D&C procedure. She made up some story, telling the neighbors that I hadn't left any diapers for my son. I came home while hemorrhaging and devastated to this woman in my ear about not leaving diapers. I have to put out yet another fire while I am physically, emotionally, and mentally exhausted.

Now, I know while growing up, my grandmother was my superhero, but you know how when you get older, you start seeing your elders through more mature eyes? I loved that woman to pieces, but she was as messy as they came. She would make up stories for no reason just to get stuff started. She would dabble in my and my mom's relationships, telling lies to our husbands and trying to bring division, saying that they didn't need us and that they were too good for us. On some level, I think she did this as a tactic to get them out of our lives because she didn't want us with them, but her way of going about things was a little backwards. She was even quick to gossip about me and my mom to our spouses. It's still hard for me to fault her, though, because her own background was full of trauma and abuse.

My grandmother was one of ten kids. One of her brothers even became the famous jazz singer, "Little Jimmy Scott." Though he is now deceased, his music lives on through sources such as episode 25 in season two of The Cosby Show.

Though my grandmother and her siblings were a talented bunch, they faced hardship early on when their mother was killed in a car accident. Subsequently, they dispersed into the foster care system. As a result, my grandmother was exposed to a lot at a young age and endured harsh circumstances that caused her to be tough as nails. I understood that her ways of lying and manipulating were out of her unhealed trauma. I've always seemed to have a gift to empathize with victims of abuse, even when they function in unhealthy ways. I think, for me, love trumps all, and I know that my grandmother and my mother loved me. I just think that my mother struggled with self-love, which is why she never left my father. But self-love was something else we didn't talk about back then. Who had time for self-love when trying to dodge a fist to the eye or an onslaught of daily putdowns?

So, when my grandmother was coming at me crazy on those stairs the day I returned from losing my boys, and my body was still dispelling their existence, I did what I always did. I became the adult in the situation. I retrieved my son and pushed myself to care for him. The days passed by, and inevitably, grief tailed me like a shadow I couldn't get rid of. Inky black darkness became the lens through which I filtered life. I was disappointed in myself. Why couldn't I seem to carry boys? I had learned my pregnancies with boys were so difficult because of the RH factor, which caused my body to attack the fetus' blood cells since their blood was RH positive and mine was RH negative. I knew this logically, but my heart was broken.

Still, I could not let my grief stop me. I had responsibilities. My child was dependent on me. Though I was technically on welfare, I found a way to work two jobs and bring in more income while my grandmother watched my son. I was making the best out of my situation with my ex-husband because I wasn't ready to let him go, even with all the red flags and his diagnosis. I loved that man so much and truly believed things could get better. Sadly, they would not until I finally left.

There was a time when my ex was in the Navy, and my son and I lived with him in Gulfport, Mississippi. My ex was in a part of the Navy, where he would reside stateside for seven months and then be out of the country for seven months. During the seven months he was stateside, I would move down to Gulfport, Mississippi, and live with him. I had decided that I wouldn't live there on my own while he was out of the country because I didn't feel safe there, and I didn't know anyone. When I wasn't living with him, my son and I stayed with my grandmother in East Cleveland or my mom's back in Cleveland Heights.

At one point, my ex-husband kicked me and my one-year-old son out of our home in Mississippi, all because I left a dish out or had done something else minor that he didn't like. When he went to physically assault me, my son jumped on him. He then threw us both down on the ground and proceeded to tell us to get out. He kicked us out of the house right there in Gulfport, Mississippi, where we knew no one! At that point, I contacted my grandmother, and she got us a room at the Navy Lodge and plane tickets to come home to Cleveland. But still, I couldn't let him go. It was bad, but apparently, it hadn't gotten bad enough.

It was in this misguided state of holding onto the marriage that I intentionally became pregnant again. This time it was a girl. Thank God it was a girl. It turns out the hyperemesis gravidarum only comes on the scene when I'm pregnant with boys, so I finally caught a break with my pregnancy. At least, outside of the 25 hours of labor, placenta previa, and being induced early! Having my daughter was a beacon of light. Both of my children are beacons of light. I couldn't have pushed forward through the awful abuse I was experiencing and the frequent affliction to my body from cancer that I would endure without knowing that I had to create a better future for them.

There was one thing that was initially a struggle after having my children: feeling like it wasn't safe to allow them to be around my father. I was mostly concerned about my daughter because I knew my father didn't mess with boys. Once the abuse started, I never felt secure or safe as a child alone with him, and I wanted to make sure they had the safety I never had. The interesting thing is that my dad treated my son better than he had ever treated me. I would find him fixing after-school snacks for him, and flashbacks of the numerous times I would be forced to make my own snacks would surface. My daughter, on the other hand, really wanted nothing to do with my father. She would look at him and then walk the other way. After a few years, I was assured that both of my children were protected. They would not have the horrible violations that I experienced, and that let me know life could get better. Life would get better. It would just take time.

One thing about me is that I refuse to be the victim. Instead, I view myself as an innocent bystander in someone else's story. I was the innocent bystander in my father's story. I was the innocent bystander in my ex-husband's story. I was an innocent bystander to Hodgin's Lymphoma, not once, but twice. But I refused to let the darkness of these atrocities be my identity. Though I was subjected to abuse, I knew deep down I was worth so much more, and I knew without a doubt that my children were, too. It would be that deep-rooted belief that would propel me forward to discover just who I was in the face of unprecedented adversity. And that belief would be my secret weapon in fighting cancer.

"My mother nurtures with a true passion and has been instrumental to the man I have become. The life lessons came fast but always had deeper meaning than the surface. She is the embodiment of willpower. There has yet to be any obstacle be it professional or personal that can stop her."
- London (her son)

"My experience with my friend/sister Staci K AKA PurPose has been nothing short of inspiring. Despite the challenges that she continues to face each day with courage, and a sense of hope reminds me of how resilient the human spirit can be. Her infectious smile and positive outlook on life are motivation for me to keep going despite my own challenges. I love her whole being."
- Tonya Craig

CHAPTER 7: SUPERWOMAN

Anytime you're diagnosed with cancer, you have to get follow-up appointments every six months. That's what I had been doing for years, and for years, I was in the clear. I was living my best little life. I was advancing in my career. I had managed to scale the ladder of success while mustering up the courage to leave my broken marriage. By the time I hit 30, I was a Director of a major hospital, overseeing 52 employees and three supervisors in the accounts receivables department. I was putting my snazzy diploma in Medical Assisting from Remington College to good use and then some. The college was so impressed with me finishing my program while battling cancer that they gave me an award. That is something I can say about my life; in the face of difficult circumstances, I thrive.

Attending Remington landed me an internship, and that internship led to a job. Remember I said before that I never went to a four-year college because I never needed to? It was the same with Remington. When I was released into the working world, I flourished and got hired fast because their education only confirmed what I already knew. I was a natural. When I transitioned into the working world after my internship, I started out in collections, working in clinical and billing and cleaning up old past due accounts. Eventually, I moved into cash application. That's where things became interesting. One other associate and I were assigned to pilot an automatic cash application system, which ultimately replaced our manual labor of applying monies. They basically had us replace ourselves with a computer system. Well, that meant I needed another position. No worries. I ended up in a lead position in a different department. I was there for a while, but there was no upward mobility. If you haven't already guessed, I'm an ambitious person. I need to be challenged and on the go. Part of this is a good thing. Work is and has always been a great outlet for the craziness circling the other areas of my life. But part of it is an escape. If I'm working, I can't sit with myself. If I'm working, I can't dwell on the hard parts of life. I've never been a dweller. When you've dealt with the levels of abuse and trauma that I have, you can't afford to be. You won't make it. So the things I could not control, my father, my ex-husband, and my body, were all put on the back burner when I was working. I was my own superhero when I was working.

After the cash application job fizzled I worked at a different company in accounts receivables and became a lead in my department within two months' time. Within a year I was a manager over Patient Relations and the Help Desk. Within two years I became a Director.

In my personal life, I was back at writing and even published my first pamphlet. I mean book. I say pamphlet because that's what my son called it, but to me, it was 20 pages of brilliance. Look out, Nobel Prize! With that book, I was creating a blueprint for women to start over, having no idea that I was preparing to do the same. I was writing my own exit strategy from my crazy marriage well before I even left it. Isn't it like that sometimes? God puts purpose into our hearts, but we're not fully aware of that purpose, so we kind of dance around it or unknowingly walk in it? So that's what was happening. I was dancing in purpose.

We bought a house in Euclid with my ex-husband's benefits around that time. The kids were going to school there, and I was happy about that because prior to that, we lived in the inner city, and the school they attended was featured on the local news every night. And not in a good way. It served as an example of why Cleveland needed to get the school levy (at the time) passed ASAP. The school was so bad that literal holes gaped down from the ceilings. I started showing up every day as a volunteer because I was so concerned for my kids' welfare. They were only five and eight years old. Well, I showed up so much the principal gave me a job as a parent and community liaison and as her administrative assistant. The school was a culture shock, to say the least. I had always been a bit bougie, and my son had attended a suburban school beforehand, so when I became a flying helicopter parent, it may have seemed strange to some, but my behavior was a reflection of what I knew we were called to be as a family. We were not called to this level of roughness, and if we were going to be in that situation, then I was going to be a change agent in the situation. Anytime I enter a room it's with the intent to change it for the better. If I can't change it, then it's not the room for me. I worked my butt off there, creating after-school programs and a school choir in addition to being the principal's right hand. The environment bloomed with life and positivity. I saw a need and met it, which was just one indicator of my calling into entrepreneurship.

That time of working at the school came to an end though when I went into the corporate world, but I brought it up because one day, something significant happened there. I was playing hooky from work (at that point, I was in corporate), deciding I needed a day off, and ended up going to the school to visit friends who worked there. There I am, shooting the breeze, thinking I'm taking a much-needed mental health day, and the secretary tells me that I have a phone call. Who in the world is calling me here when I no longer work here? And who could know I'm here? I'm thinking as I take the phone. It turns out my grandmother had a stroke, and the hospital called me at the school because the only contact information my grandmother had was my name and old job information on a card. It was a divine moment. If I had not taken that day off work for a mental health day, which was rare in and of itself, and then decided to go up to my old job at the school and then be there at that exact moment, I would not have gotten that call. That is the hand of God in my life. These are the bright lights that shine exuberantly, shouting that I am not alone. They were shouting that my grandmother was not alone, too, and she desperately needed encouragement. She was still a busybody, up to her old tricks of causing drama and chaos. The house we were living in in the hood actually belonged to her, yet when she purchased it, she told my ex-husband that he and the kids could live there. Mind you, she mentioned nothing about me living there but only that he and the kids could stay there. Well, we all moved in, and she moved in with her brother, the Jazz musician. Her brother ended up kicking her out because she was being her typical messy self and starting drama between him and his girlfriend, so she moved in with us. Now, we are all one big happy family living under one roof, but of course, it couldn't last because my ex-husband was avoiding this mental health issue that he wouldn't get help for. He and I were constantly in and out of separation.

During one period of separation, I was traveling a lot for work, so it was common for my grandmother to watch the kids during the week while I was gone. For some reason, my ex got it in his head that he had sole custody of the kids because, of course, my grandmother is letting him stay there and think about this while I'm traveling for work. One night at 2 am, he called me, threatening to end his life, saying that he wanted to tell me goodbye before he did so. I started freaking out because he's at the house with my kids, and I didn't want them exposed to and dealing with that type of trauma. I tried talking him off the ledge, but he kept going on and on about ending his life. I knew at this point he was on drugs and drinking, but I wasn't privy to how bad the drug usage was. The fear was escalating in me, and I couldn't get him to calm down, so I finally decided to get in the car and drive to my grandmother's home; luckily, I had gotten back in town earlier that day and was resting at home when he called. I found him on the porch with a 40-ounce of Old English in one hand and a gun in the other. My grandmother's car was parked in the driveway with the music blasting (she had been letting him drive her car back and forth to work). I tried to get him to turn it down; after all, by this time, it was

3 in the morning, but he refused. Frustrated with his refusal to turn it down after asking him multiple times to do so, he actually pointed the gun in my direction and shot at me! Thank God he missed, but my children were in the house, and my grandmother was in the doorway. I yelled for her to go in the house to keep them safe and hurried back to my car. My grandmother claimed she was going to call the police, but she never did. She felt bad for him, and as a result, his behavior went without consequence.

That near-death experience with him was a new one for me. My ex-husband had physically and verbally assaulted me, but never had he shot a gun at me. My life should have ended then because I was only a few feet away from him. It was the mercy of God on my life. It was another divine moment. But still, I stayed in the marriage. I stayed and focused on work. I focused on writing. I focused on purpose, but he was determined to tear me down.

One day, I came home and found the laptop and printer I used to print my book both destroyed. I knew he had done it because he saw me thriving. I had been selling my book, gaining my strength, and gathering my courage, and it scared the mess out of him. In my typical fashion, I found another outlet. I used my work computer to print my book. I would not be stopped. I was growing in confidence. Men who had either been flirting the whole time and I had just never noticed or who were attracted to my newfound confidence started popping up. I went out and found out I was hot, and that was the beginning of the end. I was back to getting phone numbers everywhere I went, even at the gas station. Folks were feeling me.

One day, I came home and found the laptop and printer I used to print my book both destroyed. I knew he had done it because he saw me thriving. I had been selling my book, gaining my strength, and gathering my courage, and it scared the mess out of him. In my typical fashion, I found another outlet. I used my work computer to print my book. I would not be stopped. I was growing in confidence. Men who had either been flirting the whole time and I had just never noticed or who were attracted to my newfound confidence started popping up. I went out and found out I was hot, and that was the beginning of the end. I was back to getting phone numbers everywhere I went, even at the gas station. Folks were feeling me. I had known this before my ex but lost it along the way with all his degrading insults. I started seeing who I was, and I could see that he saw it too and he was scared. But just when I was about to make my exit, I got the news. During one of those six-month check-in follow-up appointments I had to do for Hodgkin's Lymphoma, I found out the cancer was back. I was re-diagnosed. My world began to spin. My stomach dropped. My plans for independence crumbled. And just when I thought I was finally about to be free, there it was. Another bout with cancer.

"As I've gotten to know PurPose over the years. I see her name is fitting because she operates in her PurPose. She is the epitome of a Boss. I've never seen anyone with the work ethic, passion, and drive she has while facing the adversity of Cancer. She is the definition of a warrior. She has a personality that's infectious and a gift she shares with the world.
~Nissay Harris

CHAPTER 8: KEEP IT MOVING

If you haven't been in a domestic abusive relationship, it may seem confusing or even off-putting that I gave my ex so many chances. But too many women can relate to that kind of attachment, especially in intimate partner abuse cases. Clinical psychologists attest that domestic abuse victims' brains become altered to resemble those who have fought in military wars. The PTSD that impacts abuse victims is the same PTSD that affects military soldiers. So when a woman is in a cycle of jumping in and out of a relationship with her abuser or struggles to leave at all, it is because her brain has formed an attachment to them, one that has become, in a sense, like a drug addiction. That means kicking the habit of addiction to an abuser is the equivalency of kicking the habit of cocaine. Sometimes, crack cocaine. This is because, in the aftermath of those who successfully leave abusive situations, something that is called trauma bonding occurs. Trauma bonding is frequently misconstrued in pop culture as a bond formed between two individuals who experience a traumatic event together, but that is incorrect. Instead, trauma bonding is the bond/attachment a victim forms to his or her abuser. Add this phenomenon to my history of child and sexual abuse and you can understand even more why this toxic relationship was, on some level, normal to me. It was familiar, and we humans commonly gravitate to what is familiar.

The times when my ex and I were separated would be short-lived because my brain wasn't able to fully detox him due to these trauma bonds. The love bombing he would do would be interwoven in the toxicity. There were times he would be super nice and take me on dates. We would get dressed up, and he would pay me compliments, but that type of behavior wouldn't even last the whole day, and the monster within would eventually surface. He would do the same kind of behavior with the kids and basically, just build them up to let them down. That yoyo mistreatment was forming the bonding in my brain, and chemically, I was attached. He was also too much in my life for me to stay away, mostly as a result of having children with him and sometimes even because my grandmother was allowing him to live with her. I, of course, don't fault her, as I previously explained, because I understood her dysfunction.

That's probably why I let her move in with us when she got kicked out of her brother's home. I knew she was a kind-hearted soul who had been dealt a bad hand. The drama that ensued with her in the house, though, I'm sure, only caused my level of anxiety to increase. There were times she would go around telling her siblings that she was forced to pay our bills. Those were bold-faced lies. There was one thing my ex-husband was absolutely going to do, and that was pay the bills. We may not have had anything in the fridge to eat, but we were going to have the bills paid. It wasn't until later that we found out my grandmother was dealing with mini strokes that aided in her failing mental health. Poor thing struggled until the day she died in a nursing home.

On my personal health front, my second diagnosis of cancer was met with the same callous, uncaring attitude from my ex-husband as the first one. Even though we were now living in a nicer neighborhood in the house he purchased with his military benefits, things were rocky. His mental health was plummeting, as seen in the very walls he destroyed in our home. Yes, this man literally knocked out the walls. He claimed he was going to rebuild and make the curved hallway arch in our house into a square. This wasn't a farfetched notion since he did construction in the military. The problem was that as the days, weeks, and months rolled by, there stood a gaping hole that allowed any passersby to peer from the second floor straight into the basement. Our home was a great depiction of the chaos around us. Every day, my children and I were faced with this terrorist who found some kind of way to belittle us, disrespect us, and make our lives miserable. He was a classic narcissist through and through, and even his own flesh and blood couldn't inspire him to be a decent human being. There were times my children would be sitting in the house hungry, and he would buy food for himself and eat it in front of them, not giving a damn about anyone but himself. Or he would purchase ice cream sandwiches and gobble them down and not offer them any. Being bipolar has nothing to do with being as selfish as#hole. This was narcissism through and through.

On top of the foolishness of deconstructing the house, my ex decided he wanted to be polygamous. I may have put up with a lot from him, but having sister wives was not going to be on that list. I had a few rules on the table: no extra wives, no baby mamas, and no more kids. He wanted more children, but I had gotten my tubes tied. There was no way I was going through another horrendous pregnancy fighting for my life from hyperemesis gravidarum. I was already fighting for my sanity and sometimes physical safety living with him. I was already fighting to heal from another round of cancer.

Dealing with that second diagnosis was tough by itself, but to add to it, I had all that personal stuff going on. The other thing is I was dependent on my ex's health insurance. I wrestled with that one. Initially, I felt imprisoned in my circumstances. I had finally gotten the courage to make my exit from the house of horrors, but now it felt like I needed him financially. In the end, I knew there was just no way I would be able to stay in that home and heal from my second diagnosis. I gathered my courage and my things and moved out. I chose to leave my children there so they could attend the good suburban school they were in, but they were adamant they were coming with me. They would have rather slept on a rock-hard floor, in the corner of a room, in the inner city, than in the house with that man.

That's the part that breaks my heart, though. I had already had a rough situation with my father. My desire was to give my kids a good father and yet it was more of the same. I had managed to keep them from the sexual abuse, but I still could not keep them from the emotional and verbal abuse. They would have to learn how to deal with toxicity in the home, just as I had. What I will say is my son was like me and flourished in the face of adversity. He grew up fast and assumed the role of the little man in the house, often taking care of his little sister and making sure she was good. Even at times, taking care of me. I always tell my son that he grew up with me. Because I had him so young, we were both young, and I was maturing just as he was. I think that resulted in his maturing even faster. He just seemed to be emotionally in tune with my needs, even when I hadn't told him about the re-diagnosis. I told very few about it because I didn't want my mom to worry, and there simply weren't many I could depend on. I was even taking myself to my own doctor's appointments. I ended up telling my best friend, who was also my employee at the time because I needed her to cover for me if I went to work late after getting treatments. I made sure to schedule my treatments either before or after work so that I wasn't missing too much work. That just lets you know how dedicated I was to my career.

I successfully had the treatments scheduled with as little inconvenience as possible, but the thing about chemotherapy is you're always nauseous, and I already told you the struggle I had with the nausea medication, so I couldn't control that part. Thankfully, my best friend was a saint and kept me a stash of salt and vinegar potato chips that worked wonders for my nausea. I would go to work after those treatments, salivating at the mouth! Those chips got me through four months of treatment and two months of infusions. Still, chemo is very aggressive on the organs. The very thing that can help you can hurt you. As I mentioned before, a side effect is sudden death. This time around I also had hair loss. It wasn't noticeable to others, but we know our bodies. I filled in the thinning areas with pieces of weave and, like I always do, kept it moving.

Throughout all of this, as usual, my ex was MIA, but I didn't feel personally let down by it. I handled my business, made sure to take care of my kids, and got the assistance I needed to heal. By the time I moved out, it was clear to me that he and I were not just on two different pages but in two different books entirely. He was tearing down our home while I was building up my temple. Everywhere he went, there was destruction and chaos. Everywhere I went, my environment bloomed. When I moved out, I decided I would not allow his idiocracy to defeat me. I would not allow cancer to defeat me. I was determined to win.

"I've known this Warrior for over 20 years. Her faith in God, strength, and determination always amazes me. She continues to win and help others win no matter what life throws her way and she does it with grace."
- Michelle Cole

"The first time I met Staci her presence was unforgettable. Standing confidently in a vibrant hot pink dress, she embraced her silhouette without a breast prosthesis, embodying a bold fearlessness that left the audience in awe. Her strength and authenticity set the stage for a connection that would forever inspire me."
- Denise M. West

CHAPTER 9: ONE HOT CADILLAC

The thing about Hodgkin's Lymphoma that's different from other cancers is that it's highly recurrent. That means even when it's gone, its threat lurks in the background for the rest of your life, like a bully you thought you had already beaten up in middle school. Sometimes bullies need to be beaten up a few times before they figure out you're not one to mess with.

Before that second diagnosis, I was living my best little life. I was coming into my own, diving into the waters of writing and creativity, scaling the heights of corporate America, and playing both mom and dad to my children. I was even hosting girlfriend brunches and lunches for women based on my book, where I presented speakers and vendors and topics of discussion on healing and self-growth. Not many people in the community were doing that type of work back then. As much as it annoyed me, it was clear my purpose involved women's empowerment even when I kept trying to run from it. Women always seemed to flock to me. I would tell God, "Stop giving me women!" but He would keep on until I finally relented. This was an exciting experience, though, that I got to share with my mom, my best friend, and my amazing kids who would support and help me plan events. We were really gaining traction in the community.

Having found my purpose made the difficulty of dealing with cancer more bearable, but I was still mad as hell when it reemerged, threatening all of my plans to leave the monster I was married to. Still, I could not focus on what I could not change. All I could do was set out to change what I could, which was my mindset and perspective. I also had the blessing of having my children as my prime motivation. I was all they had.

As I said earlier, the hardest part of that time wasn't just the cancer; it was watching my children suffer at their father's hands. My son was always large for his age and, as a result, wasn't able to play peewee football. He loved football, but because of his size, the coaches didn't allow him to play. That put him behind in getting the experience he would need to advance in the sport. So, who was out there teaching him how to tackle? That would be me while his father sat inside the house watching TV.

When my son made the team in high school, I was at every game, while his father never even attended one. I was cheering my kids on, being both mom and dad, but that was the example I had growing up. My father was a leach and didn't contribute one lick to the household in any shape or form. My mother was the financial provider. My mother was the emotional support. My mother was the one doing it all. When it came to the sexual abuse, she dropped the ball. She never kicked him out because he never admitted his wrongdoing, but she always said that if he was wrong and he really did do what he denied doing, it would catch up to him, and he would suffer. She was right. By the end of his life, my father ended up being tormented with guilt. He called out several times while in the hospital bed, in fear that I was there coming to kill him along with the imaginary demons he was seeing. He told my mother I was there to get my revenge. I was nowhere in that room; it was just his own guilt eating him alive.

By then, he could barely see due to diabetic retinopathy and, in a divine set of ironic circumstances, was an impotent shell who could scarcely move. My mom was his lifeline. But all of his evilness caught up to him by the end of his life after letting a sore go unattended on his foot. By the time the doctors found it, sepsis had set in, and it was too late. Ultimately, this was a result of complications from his diabetes. He was stuck in the house until he died in the hospital and was, in a sense, a prisoner in his own home.

During my father's decline, all I could do was shake my head at the pathetic version of himself he had withered to. This once predatory man had turned weak, but thankfully, by then, I had forgiven him. I had arrived at some kind of peace about our past and kept things cordial because, at the end of the day, I still wanted a relationship with my dad. Outside of his abuse, he was actually a fun guy. He was funny and charismatic and could make any heavy situation lighter with colorful, comical sayings, in addition to an unusual knack for making up cuss words. He was always telling hilarious stories (all lies), but he did it in such a funny way that you couldn't even be mad that they were lies. He was easy to like, and if someone didn't know his deep, dark secret, then they wouldn't have a clue. That's why the molestation was such a disappointment. Before then, I had held him in high regard.

After he died, I moved in with my mom, and soon after, the kids came to live with us. My ex spiraled even more, and his drug addiction was at an all-time high. One day, I visited the house in Euclid and realized it had turned into a bonafide trap house. I was like, "Who are all these people?" having no idea that they were either drug dealers or drug users. I really was, for a long time, naive about his drug usage. He ended up getting kicked out of the military after going AWOL. This was a double loss for the family because, at the time, the Navy was offering us a house we wouldn't have to pay rent for in Virginia, where he was stationed. It was like he was self-sabotaging and foregoing the blessing he could have been to our family. Instead of making things better, he kept making them worse. The Navy slapped a "dishonorable discharge" on his record, coupling it with a mental health disorder. On top of him losing his job, he lost the home in Euclid and the dog and became homeless. I had pity on him and let him stay in a spare room in our home, though I made it clear this was a temporary situation and that he wasn't getting any extra luxuries. The room didn't even have a bed. So he was back, and we were all under one roof yet again. I was navigating my treatments, but this time, I switched hospitals. With us no longer having military insurance and due to the previous mishaps, I felt a change was needed. But even with that switch, the process was grueling. There is just no way around it. Everything about cancer is hard. The harshness of the treatment on your body. The weariness that sets in not just in your physical being but in your soul. The never-ending poking and prodding. It was all I could do to keep it moving.

My children were the greatest reason to fight. Around this time, my son was a senior attending prom. His father promised that he could borrow his fancy money green Cadillac to escort his date. The day of prom arrives, my ex is nowhere to be found, and neither is his precious Caddy. His disappearance was not atypical, however; he would often be gone for days only to resurface with no explanation. The issue was that now he was pulling this at the expense of my son's prom experience. I called him like crazy, blowing him up, but no answer. I called his best friend, who said he hadn't seen him, but I didn't believe him. I went looking for him at his friend's house and saw his parked Caddy in the driveway. I start banging on the door and his best friend answers, making up lies, saying he hadn't seen him, yet the man's car is parked at his home. Something tells me to look inside the car. Right there, smack dab in broad daylight, are two naked chocolate bodies lying one over the other across the front seats. I start knocking on the passenger side window. A female looks up, startled and blinking. Her face immediately turns to horror once she realizes what is happening.

"Open the door," I say, and then I ask the first question that pops into my brain. "Why are you butt-naked in the car with somebody's husband?" Maybe it was the shock of it all because even though at that point we *were* legally married, that man and I had been divorced for a while in my heart. Nevertheless, that's what spilled out of my mouth. She had the nerve to answer, "Oh! Because it was hot," as if that made all the sense in the world. Now, this just lets you know where I was with things because I did not yell. I did not scream. I did not try to fight this woman. Instead, I watched her slip on her clothes, scurry out of the vehicle, and somehow get the garage door open to hide inside. I would have laughed if I wasn't so livid that my son was the one being harmed by my ex's foolishness. My ex then had the nerve to open his mouth and start talking. "You see how these B's lie! That's not why she was naked," as if the woman was the only one in the wrong. I didn't care what he had to say; all I needed was his car and his money. Even though he was a certified vagabond, he had some money left from his 401K and had received thousands of dollars after being let go. Not to mention, he was also receiving military benefits as well. "Your son needs money and the car for prom," I reminded him through gritted teeth. He offered to take me to the bank to get the money, but that would mean me being in his filthy vehicle, and I needed it sanitized before that would ever happen. There was no *way* I was getting in that thing.

Later that day, he appeared at the house with the car and his bike so he could commute to wherever he was going afterward. I offered him a ride, but for some reason, he said "no" and instead asked if I could drop off some of his clothes at a hotel. After sending my baby off to his prom, I started calling my ex to get him his clothes, but he didn't answer. I popped up at the hotel anyway and heard loud reggae music blasting from one of the rooms, a telltale sign that he was there. My ex loved Reggae. After I knocked on the door, who else was there to greet me but the very woman I had found him with earlier that day in his car?

She is startled as I enter and see him looking unbothered, jamming to his music. But instead of me flipping out or going crazy, I do something that is the epitome of who I am and what I am called to do. I started ministering to this woman.

"Do you have children? Don't you know you're better than this?" The woman is in tears. She nods her head low, ashamed, admitting she has four kids. "Where are your children?" I am asking, my heart bursting with concern. This woman's poor choices that led her into these circumstances are my primary concern, not my ex's clear-cut adultery. Unlike most women in my shoes, I'm not even viewing her as an enemy. Instead of anger, all I have is compassion. I offered to give her a ride out of this man's vices. She kept looking at him, but he didn't care about one scent. He just continued bobbing to his music and dancing. I'm sad to say she didn't take me up on my offer. I left that room alone that day. But even though *she* didn't take the way of escape, I realized that I had. I was choosing a different road than her. It didn't make me better, but because I had the courage to leave my ex, my self-value was restored. Now I was in a place to offer to bring other women with me. Even if they were sleeping with my husband.

"Humility, Innovation, Selflessness, and Strength serve up just a small portion of what This WARRIOR brings to the universe. I'm here for it all!"
~Coach Sass

CHAPTER 10: FLYING, NO PARACHUTE

Once I made it over the hurdle of Hodgkin's Lymphoma the second time, I got back to the business of living my best little life. I was knee deep into the poetry scene by then and became a frequent performer at open mics throughout the city. Poetry had always been my go-to healing balm for pain. It was what woke me up to my pain as an adolescent, wrapping safe arms around me and shielding me with lyrical rhythms. It did the job my parents could not when my home was a day-to-day nightmare I yearned to wake up from. Poetry was always there for me, and unlike my wayward ex, it never let me down.

The poetry scene was another avenue where my entrepreneurial spirit kicked in. After noticing all the men hosting, I saw an opportunity to host open mics myself. My open mics were legendary! I wanted people to be immersed in art and freedom. Bright colors, artistic sculptures, and paintings graced the environment. I also gave complimentary wine to my guests and didn't charge for my open mics. I wanted my events to be a welcome place to come and share for both seasoned poets and newbies. The men of Chief Rocka Entertainment, a group of poets who held the longest-running open mic in Cleveland, supported me 200%! They respected what I was doing and showed up. To my knowledge, no other women at the time were doing this. I was always the one in my family willing to fly without a parachute, so though it was a risky move, I jumped. After I opened that door, a few women started doing open mics, and I was front and center supporting their events as they had done mine!

One thing about me is if I see it, I feel like I can do it myself. I accredit this staunch belief system to my independence as a child. A benefit to growing up with no one telling you "no" is that you don't believe that there is anything you *can't* do.. This was the positive aspect of being a latchkey kid whose mom was always working and plagued with guilt about her husband's abuse. The negative consequence was that I had a hard time with leadership. I hardly paid my bosses any mind and instead desired to "do me." But even that little flaw would become a benefit because, in the end, I was called to be my own boss.

Though I can be inspired by what is, I also have an innate drive to create what is not. On top of that, I then want to strap others in with me on the ride of pioneering. That's what happened when I led open mics; I pioneered female leadership in an untapped arena and brought my people with me. My mom, bestie, and my heartbeats (my children) were all on my team of purpose and creativity!

Initially, we started out monthly, but then the demand grew, so we went to weekly. I got to the point where I was even paying featured poets. This was a big deal. The term "starving artist" exists for a reason, and poets don't always receive payment for their work. We had the support of the community, too, because back then, when one person was leading an open mic, we would all show up to that open mic and make sure ours wasn't scheduled on the same night. This eliminated a competitive mindset and instead fostered unity in the community. Doing it this way ensured there was no conflict for the crowd to choose who to support. They could patronize us all!

Cleveland is a city riddled with "silos." So even though it's a metropolitan area with over 350,000 residents, it harbors small pockets of the same folks in specific spaces. That means it's easy for competition to emerge in any given industry. I count it an honor to be among those breaking down the walls of disunity. That characteristic of my work and calling is threaded throughout all that I've done. Whether it was women empowerment, one-on-one coaching, or the creative space of hosting open mics, I wanted to spread hope and empowerment within the city. I even ended up teaching children creative writing and performance poetry. I was invited by a community member who owned a building, and I would teach classes there. Sometimes, if there was no available space, I would even teach kids in my home. We had a time, and I look back fondly on those moments. I developed such close relationships with the kids that even outside of class, they would call and text me about things happening outside of poetry. One of the young men who had shown immense vocal talent went on to become a famous backup singer for Erykah Badu! Giving back to those kids was like nurturing my younger self.

It wasn't long before another love entered my life. This person was a true friend of my son and was doing for him what his father should have been doing.

Spending time with him, bonding, taking him to strip clubs, and giving him the outlets for male activities that he needed. For years, I watched their budding relationship with grateful eyes, having no idea that there was also a romantic interest in me. But eventually, our relationship transitioned into an intimate space, and I fell in love. It was a love I had never experienced before. It was selfless and giving, and supportive. After the trauma of my ex and a few short-lived relationships, I was enthralled. Before this experience, I thought love was a man putting me down, putting his hands on me, or diminishing my value in some way, shape, or form. I had inherited this outlook from my dear mother. She had married another man after my father's passing, and that man wasn't any better. I would find out later that he would leave the house to do God knows what as she lay helpless on the floor for hours after having fallen. It's sad that my mother had this knack for choosing men who needed her but who were MIA when she needed them. For my mother, I have always been "her person." She could never rely on any man to offer her the same support she provided them. This wasn't love. This was codependency. This was abuse. This wasn't what we were created to be recipients of. Love is uplifting, affirming, and giving. That's what I found in my partner.

After escaping the stronghold of my ex and knocking out that old bully Hodgkin's Lymphoma a second time, I continued on purpose. I was evolving in my identity. I was finally romantically being loved in the way I deserved. I was thriving in my career. But in my late 30s, I started seeing some shifting taking place at work. I was sitting pretty in my position, but my superiors were dropping like flies. Leadership was getting out, and I knew enough to know that this was a bright red flag waving in the sky. After 16 years of being there, it was time to jump ship. I took a leap of faith and applied for a job I really didn't think I would land simply because the salary I asked for was extravagant. To my surprise, after the first interview, I was hired. They loved me. I went in as a billing manager and was promoted in six months. I became a director, overseeing all office managers, the scheduling team, and the front staff. I ended up being promoted again. I was killing it. In one month alone, I collected over $1 million. This had never been done at this company. All seemed to be on the up and up.

Finally, I was free. I was soaring. I was no longer bogged down by my crazy ex's shenanigans. I was no longer held back by verbal assaults and putdowns. I was using all of my God-given gifts and talents to meet the objectives of this company and serve my community.

Now, some of the stuff I faced at work wasn't peaches and cream. I was a Black woman in leadership in corporate America, after all. The microaggressions, stereotypes, and blatant racism were always rearing their ugly heads. I was unfairly given tasks that my white counterparts were not. I sat on the monthly owners'/board meetings where I had to present pages of information to the owners while other people on my level were given an "ok" to pass on sharing anything from their departments. I was advised by an amazing friend and coworker that I was the lowest-paid executive, yet I had the most employees under me and in most departments. But I had overcome more than any mere corporate racists could throw my way. I was a 3x cancer survivor, dammit! Didn't they know who they were messing with? Still, what I didn't know was that my boxing rounds with cancer weren't over. In fact, they had just begun. This time, my opponent would take on a different form. While Hodgkin's Lymphoma was temporarily knocked down, with a white flag waving, another form of cancer would emerge and take its best shot.

In 2018, at the age of 44, I was diagnosed with breast cancer.

MENTAL CLEANSE
Taken from "Soul of PurPose" by Staci PurPose Kirk 2009

Dreams of what hope springs
Eternal
Leaving the negative behind giving positive its place
Internal
What you think you see of me
External
Keeping safe the prophetic voice inside my
Journal
Breathing life into thoughts of better days
Fundamental
Ignorance runs bliss ...so I turn my back to the **Judgmental**
Embracing life as the gift it is and treating it as mine **Beneficial**
An angel guards the door of my mind as I flow -my **Sentinel**
The enemy takes clever strides to corrupt the blessed
Criminal
Small deposits of strength through vibes
Subliminal
Reality through the education of my own mistakes
Forgivable
Instilling streams of conscious awakening
Commendable
Lessening and degrading ideology of negativity
Expendable
Cognizant of society's power trips and stereotypes **Intolerable**
Praying blessings of abundant edifications surge
Plentiful
Internalizing the soul's seeing inside mirror
Beautiful
Fervently falling to my knees
Prayerful
That God will enable me to again cleanse my
MENTAL

"Even if there isn't a song in her heart, she sings anyway! Staci's diligence, bravery, strength, and fighting spirit is something I will always admire"
- CiCi Norris

CHAPTER 11: NOT MY BOOBS!

At 44 years old, I was the only Black female on an all-white executive team working as an operations experienced manager supervising six offices, six office managers, the front desk staff of all their offices, and a call center. I was the only brown face in a sea of white at every board meeting. The only person of color voicing a diverse perspective in secret boardroom decision-making conversations. You can imagine the weight on my shoulders as being "the only." Too often in our society, minorities are the only ones who ever experience this. Even more so while we're trying to build something sustainable for our families and communities. We have to adopt the language and culture of the one that's dominant to scale the ladder of success. We're pressured to alter our natural identity to be accepted as much as possible by our Caucasian counterparts so we can put food on the table in our homes. The C.R.O.W.N Act is a great example of the progress we're making in this area, but it took 150plus years to pass it or even acknowledge the need to. Black women's hair products are still shoved in a corner on a tiny shelf in the hair aisle of any major shopping center while the blondes' and brunettes' products languish on the rest of the shelves. Visit any well-known store and see for yourself.

Those in the majority rarely glimpse through the eyes of the only. They're rarely even aware of the subtle and subconscious hurdles we must jump over to be even considered in the race. They're rarely aware of their own privilege.

I wore my position as a badge of honor and set out to excel, not wallowing in my disadvantages but confidently seeking what I knew I was called to, and that was more. I was called to more than what my society tried to make me believe. Our family may have had our financial struggles, but we were never meant to stay there. The resiliency I had to overcome cancer, I used to overcome any obstacle that came my way, including in the workplace.

I won my team over and gained the respect of my peers. I was the go-to person for the call center associates and quickly became their designated advocate. They knew they could rely on me to hear them out and speak on their behalf if needed. It was a high-power, stressful position that carried great responsibility on top of the added responsibility of performing while Black when others were eagerly anticipating your downfall. Even still, I thrived. It was clear to all that I was the chosen superstar. It wasn't until one particular new hire came on board the executive team as the director of finance that things took a turn. When someone finds out who the superstar is and they covet that role, they plot their attack. This man didn't take kindly to the favor I had with so many. Everything I suggested, he countered. Whenever I had an idea, he would challenge it. I was badgered about things that weren't even a part of my job responsibilities. His "white is right" mindset set out to destroy the fanbase I had crafted, and he constantly slandered me to my colleagues. Every decision I made began to be questioned. Every hire or fire I made was up for debate, whereas when I first arrived, I was treated with respect and promoted twice in my first few months. This mistreatment was disheartening on so many levels. I honestly felt like the director of finance, and I could have worked well together, but he was out for himself. The sad thing is he was two kinds of ugly. He wasn't just a racist; he was a jealous racist. Jealousy for any individual is ugly, but on a grown white male, it's just pathetic. How can the most privileged person on the planet feel entitled to obtain even more?

In 2018, when I received my diagnosis of breast cancer, I was in the midst of dealing with this turmoil at work. It also came during a routine examination. I had never had a mammogram before, and the doctor I was seeing suggested I could do it that very day on a different floor of the hospital. Needless to say, I was nervous. I hadn't had a follow-up appointment in years for Hodgkins' because my results kept coming back negative, and my veins are heavily sclerosed from chemo, so injecting the IVs was always traumatic. But I trusted this doctor and finally found someone who had my best interest at heart. He knew I was afraid of the mammogram. *Not my boobs!* I'm thinking as I'm picturing them crushed by that machine that flattens them like pancakes. I'm not sure what my face looked like at his suggestion, but my doctor said words I'll never forget. "You don't have to die from not knowing something you can find out about right now." Whew! I mean, who can argue with that?

I had the mammogram done and was told I had very dense breasts. That meant I had to go to a different location and get more in-depth 3D images done. After that, I went in for an ultrasound. They found something and wanted to do a biopsy. I was a straight scaredy cat and said, "Ok, I'll be back tomorrow." I was not ready for that needle. Even though I had been put through the wringer with Hodgkins', I had hated needles since I was a kid. I took a day to let all of this new information settle and returned the next day for the biopsy. I faced the gun with the needle at the end of it as the loud clicking noise rang in my ears. They inject you twice for every sample, so I had to endure it a few times. Days later, they called me at work and said it was breast cancer.

I'll never forget that call. I was sitting at my desk in my office and being told I had breast cancer. I'm finally free from Hodgkins. I'm in the healthiest relationship I've ever been in. My kids seemed to be minimally scarred by my ex's craziness and are grown and working, living their own lives.
Why is this happening to me? Again!?

It was probably one of the few times at work I lost it. My emotions were a wreck. I couldn't stop the diagnosis from playing repeatedly in my mind.
"You have breast cancer."
Who gave these people permission to tell me something so devastating over the phone? In the middle of my workday? Aren't they supposed to call me into the hospital when it's bad news? How am I supposed to continue working?

I was sitting in the office location where I spent the most time, frozen from shock. My mind was stuck on this devastating news when an angel walked. We called her Patty Cakes. She was the front desk secretary and a pure treasure to have. The thing about Patty Cakes was she also had been battling breast cancer. The cancer had left, come back, and was spreading to her brain. In spite of this, she showed up to work every day. She frequently entered patient information wrong, but I never wrote her up because if she could go through what she was going through and come in every day, we could for sure correct her errors. Patty Cakes was a fighter, not taking the doctors' diagnosis at face value. She would fly out of town to get second and third medical opinions. She was an inspiration to us all.

When she walked into my office and found me in the state I was in, she hurried to comfort me. We were already kindred spirits because of my history with cancer, but now our connection would go to another level. It was a divine moment. The way my office was positioned, not many would have had immediate access to me because they would first see the training center and a desk for new hires. I was almost hidden, so her intentionally looking for me was even more divine. She had come in at the exact right moment after I received the call. She hugged me and declared, "We are going through this thing together!" The next day, Patty Cakes brought in a huge pink bag full of stuff I would need for chemo; ginger candy for nausea, peppermints, lip balm, a baseball cap, an inspirational book, and other items for nausea.

Once I had my mental breakdown and my pow-wow with Patty

Cakes, I did what I always do. I started strategizing for victory. Every place I ever worked, I would always get basic medical insurance, but the previous year, my partner said, "Get everything!" That meant long-term and short-term disability, FMLA, and AFLAC. That decision was vital because that meant I would still get paid after I was diagnosed. I didn't think it was needed at the time of filling out all that paperwork, but when I went through the process of treatment and healing, I was so thankful. My insurance coverage is what saved me financially because I was able to go out on FMLA. Every time I went to chemo, I was able to get financial assistance. God had aligned things ahead of time for me to have provision, knowing what was to come.

My girl Patty Cakes was on my team, rooting for me in my race to beat breast cancer. She made her husband take her to my house and delivered me the most beautiful plaque of encouragement. It read: "She thought that she could, so she did." My heart was squeezed. I was going through it, but I was encouraged. This time around, I received support from multiple sources. Unfortunately, I didn't have support from the higher-ups at work. While I was out in recovery, the finance director was sowing seeds of discord and taking every opportunity to make me look bad. When HR asked when I would return, I said in November. The finance director used that date to sway the board to terminate me on October 1st, only one month before I was to return. I was devastated.
opportunity to make me look bad. When HR asked when I would return, I said in November. The finance director used that date to sway the board to terminate me on October 1st, only one month before I was to return. I was devastated.

On top of all that, our dear Patty Cakes lost her journey with cancer just two weeks after giving me that plaque. All of her tenacity, resilience, and bright outlook vanished from my life immediately. Suddenly, and without notice, my circumstances had gone from bad to worse.

"Warrior Coach Staci is a remarkable and selfless woman driven by a spirit of excellence, inspiring and empowering women to unlock their fullest potential. Through her unwavering mentorship and motivation, she transforms lives including mine and encourages women to rise to their best selves."
~Juntyna Goodrum

CHAPTER 12: A BOOB JOB?!

Black women especially pride ourselves in our jobs, and sometimes, we let work become our identity. When I found myself without work, it was a rough time, and my identity was shaken. Who was I without my job? On top of this uncertainty was the blatant betrayal from my superiors. I spent hours upon hours, months upon months, years upon years contributing to my company's success, but when I needed them most, they kicked me when I was down. The associate who had it out for me took every opportunity to make me look bad, and that was on him. But the ones who knew me and worked with me for years allowed his lies to sway their opinion. With one phone call, they terminated my years of dedication, not even giving me the honor of a face-to-face conversation but choosing to fire me over the phone instead. That hurt. But it didn't just hurt me; it hurt them. There were several call center reps and even office staff who left the company as a result of my unjust termination. I had served as their liaison and advocate, and without me in that position, they would have more difficulty from upper management. So they left.

Thankfully, on the side, I was coaching others in building their businesses and knew from the removal of my nine-to-five, God was saying, "Do what I told you to do." He was referring to entrepreneurship. He was referring to coaching female leaders. Up until that point, I had been coaching for free. I had been doing events for free. I had been investing in my community and in others to see the transformation, but it was time to take everything to the next level.

While trying to grow my business into something sustainable, I was navigating this new diagnosis. The issue was I hated my oncologist. My doctor would negate everything that I said. If I said I was having pain in my breast after the radiology, he would minimize it and tell me that it was normal. If I said I was having bone pain from the chemo, he would say, "Oh, that's rare." It took my loved ones to be my advocate and tell them to listen to me. Everything about my situation was rare, but because he wasn't truly concerned about my health and well-being, he didn't do his due diligence in researching my history or listening to my voice. I ended up firing him after multiple rounds of being ignored. Before then, repeatedly, he dismissed my concerns. It is vital that underrepresented patients have advocates as their voice when dealing with the hospital administration. It wasn't until this particular battle that I could see clearly the racial disparities I was facing. With Hodgkin's, I was still somewhat in the dark, and it took a while for me to understand the racism occurring. I interpreted the various attitudes from workers and not receiving adequate treatment for my diagnosis as someone just having a bad day. My rose-colored glasses were on full blast but got shattered when I kept encountering this behavior with this new round of cancer. During my time of treatment for breast cancer, I learned that even those of varying sexual orientations require advocacy. Sadly, there is discrimination against the LGBTQ+ community in the health field, as well as other minorities. It is a disgusting shame that those who are already physically afflicted and suffering have to battle the prejudiced mindsets of the ones who are trained to heal them.

Given my history with cancer, you may think I would be more equipped than most to navigate it, but Hodgkin's Lymphoma isn't as aggressive as other cancers, so from that perspective, I didn't have any more of an advantage than any other breast cancer patient. I received every symptom and side effect from the treatment for breast cancer. The fatigue. Nausea. Vomiting. All that and more. But it was the extreme bone pain that was unbearable. It's so intense the bone pain literally immobilizes you. When it was really, really bad, I could be bedridden for days. Even now, I still experience bone pain. The Tamoxifen in the chemo cocktail is what causes this ongoing agonizing experience. That's one of the ways breast cancer differs from Hodgkin's. There was no Tamoxifen in the treatment for Hodgkin's; hence, there was no bone pain as a side effect.

I ended up with a lumpectomy in my right breast, but my boobs had always been oversized, so when my surgeon asked, "How happy are you with your boobs?" I hastily replied, "They're too big!" She reconstructed both my breasts and did a reduction, a silver lining in a grim situation. I had always wanted smaller breasts! When I woke up from surgery, there were suction cups attached all over my chest. It was extremely painful when the doctors removed each one of those cups. Then, they had to remove the stitches from my body. I was in so much pain.

In a best-case scenario, doctors will use the dissolvable stitches in this type of procedure, but in my case, they used the old-school threaded stitches. After the stitches are out, your body is subjected to removing various pieces of tape and glue all over your chest. The whole thing is horrible. This is only at stage 1A breast cancer, which indicates an early detection.

Once I got through surgery, I had chemo and then radiation. I was initially going to forego the chemo, but my recurrence rate was at a marker 54 on the Oncotype DX Recurrence Chart, which indicated a high probability of recurrence. Thus, the doctor recommended chemo to prevent a recurrence. As you can imagine, there wasn't a lot of rest and recovery from the surgery before I had to start chemotherapy. The chemo itself brought with it the familiar nausea, and I struggled with having an appetite. My family would argue with me about eating. I think I was just so traumatized by all the vomiting from both my experiences with cancer treatments as well as my history with hyperemesis from my pregnancies that I wasn't on it. Additionally, you lose your sex drive during treatment. Nothing about treatment is fun. I hated being bedridden, but of course, I was still a trooper and ever the worker bee. I had my loved ones bring my laptop to my bed so I could work. Of course, there were moments of depression. I hated missing out on life. My god-grandson had just been born, and I was upset I couldn't see him. I feared the future that I wouldn't live to see my son have his own children. I didn't care about losing my hair too much since I had lost it so many times before. I can rock a bald head as much as I can rock any other hairstyle. There was some backlash, though, when I would go live on social media with my bald head. The trolls would pop up and insult me, saying, "You look like a man!" but my audience would always defend me and go after them. I didn't have to say a thing. After chemo, I received radiation, which resulted in some discoloration, but other than that, I recovered well. The whole experience from beginning to end of surgery, chemo, and radiation was about six months to a year. It was a long, hard year, but I prevailed.

The interesting thing is I had absolutely no symptoms prior to my diagnosis that indicated I even had breast cancer. I didn't have any lumps, and nothing was revealed during my self-exams or doctor's exams during my physicals. It truly was a divine moment for my doctor to encourage me to get a mammogram that day because of my cancer history. Doctors who work in the healthcare field and have hearts for their patients have the power to save lives preemptively. My doctor, who aided in my discovering breast cancer, is an example of one of the good ones.

To help support me financially I received disability for about a year, but then within a few months of that running out I knew I needed something else. Entrepreneurship often takes time to achieve sustainability and though I was still working my business, I needed stable income to take care of my family. In 2020, right before the shelter from Covid became mandatory, I re-entered the workforce.

This time around, battling breast cancer, I was more supported. My kids were grown and had a better understanding of what was happening. As a result, they were able to meet my needs. I also had a loving partner who did the same. One time, I had a fever and ended up in the ER due to an infection, and my partner stayed overnight in the hospital room with me. I wasn't used to that kind of love. I was used to having to do it all on my own. I was used to having to go through the hard decision to terminate a pregnancy with twin boys due to hyperemesis gravidarum. Alone. Suddenly, all that had changed. No longer did I have the added stress of a narcissistic, abusive drug addict with a mental health disorder, who I called my husband. Now, I am going through a more aggressive battle with cancer, but now I'm not doing it alone.

That additional support was cultivating transformation in me. It was nourishing me with love, which proved to be another weapon on top of my already natural positive outlook. I had already been a force on my own, but now I had a supportive team. I knew, without a doubt, nothing could stop me. After beating breast cancer and Hodgkin's Lymphoma, I was ready to face the world like never before.

Rest in Heaven Corinne Smith

My sister, both in love and in the fight. I hold you in my heart and take you with me in every battle.

In the lowest and darkest corners of your life, He will send relief. They will cry your tears for you and celebrate your victories alongside you.
Recognize Your Angels.
- Staci PurPose Kirk

"If you have the pleasure to engage with Staci, then you already know she is a remarkable woman! Her resilience in overcoming 6 battles with cancer is matched by her dedication to pour into and uplift others. Known as the "toe steppa" because she will step on your toes to get you moving even when hers hurt! She's the definition of a warrior!"
~Khalidah France

CHAPTER 13: SIS, LET'S WIN!

Women are good at losing their identities in a job. We spend so much time giving 200% in our work that it's hard not to. So, when I first got fired, I dealt with some depression. On top of that, I decided to sue my old company for the shady way they moved with me. I went through the process of getting a lawyer and attended the first mediation, but everything about the judicial system and police departments freaks me out. I was practically breaking out in hives trying to fill out the paperwork.

Thankfully, I got through it. All that and the suit ended in a settlement because the company had paid out my long-term disability well past my termination. Since the insurance was employee-sponsored, the court attributed their payments as their way of righting the unfair way they treated me. Time passed, and being out of work never looked good on me. I had been working since age 14. Needless to say, I grew restless and anxious. I needed something to stimulate my brain. I knew I didn't want another high-powered management position, but I couldn't be a sitting duck with bills piling up. When my friend reached out about a stable 9-to-5, I jumped on it. On the side, I had various entrepreneurial endeavors that cropped up. In 2019, my best friend and I started a group called Stiletto Boss Women's Group, which created outings for women to socialize, network, and bond in sisterhood. It was a hit. We got together for drinks and laughs and just to let our hair down. The group also supported the award ceremony I created in 2012. An endeavor I had been running on my own, out of my own pocket, for years. The Stiletto Boss Awards was created to celebrate those deserving of affirmation and acknowledgment. It was intentionally designed to spotlight the names of women who normally don't get recognized. In my city, you tend to hear about the same folks over and over, yet there are so many others doing amazing things for the community. We made sure to provide a stage for those people. In 2020, Covid put a temporary halt to the women's group due to sheltering being in place, so we were all stuck in the house.

Simultaneously, only a month after being hired for my new job, our company switched from being in the office to working from home. We were all socializing on Zoom and various social media outlets, and our precious Stiletto Boss outings were a wrap. But opposition is never a deterrent for me. I will always find a way.

In August 2020, I started Let's Win Sis. I had already been calling my coaching program Let's Win Sis, so the name was familiar to those who knew me in that setting. I just needed to re-brand and build on it. Let's Win Sis was an online social media group that catered to female leaders who had either struggled with getting their entrepreneurial ideas off the ground or were burned out from several failed attempts. I would offer free tips and ideas in this group with the intent to elevate others and create a space for professional growth. We discussed specific topics like marketing, branding, utilizing social media for business, using marketing tools such as Canva, vending, overcoming imposter syndrome, crafting an elevator pitch, networking tips, and much more. This group gave me a great outlet to exercise who I was professionally and as an entrepreneur. I also had a strong support system in place to assist me with navigating it. In purpose, sometimes we're just going with the flow, doing the first thing in front of us, having no idea how that first thing will open a door for the next thing. I was still coaching for free at this point, but unbeknownst to me, Let's Win Sis was a starting point for future clients.

Due to the advantage of most people looking for a connection online during the pandemic, Let's Win Sis blew up with 20-50 folks being added to the group weekly. People poured in for the engagement and free information. Of course, there were others who tried to duplicate our program, but I stayed in character and, instead of getting upset, simply promoted these other groups within our group. Similar to when I was trying to help my exes' lover in the hotel room that day if a woman is hurting and not doing well, I will always try to encourage her, even if her actions are hurting me. My heart for women has always been for them to succeed. I figure if I've been through almost everything a woman can possibly go through (heartbreak, divorce, abuse, depression, job termination, terminal illnesses, etc....) and made it out, they can too.

On the personal front, I was living my best little life after my healing from breast cancer. I was walking every morning, working out, traveling, and being more intentional about my peace. My backyard was revamped, creating a serene ambiance full of canopies, outside furniture, two water fountains, a rock garden, and lots of greenery. I was spending time with my new god-grandson and enjoying the new title "G-Ma." I was in celebration mode and became focused on health and happiness. There is nothing like a near-death experience to awaken you to the brevity of life. After I defeated breast cancer, it was like, "Whew! I made it!" The problem was I still was having issues with my right breast. My nights became sleepless due to the pain. The breast itself looked deformed. There was an ongoing discomfort and throbbing that wouldn't leave me. At times, I could barely focus or even think. I was constantly wishing it could be removed. Please, somebody, take this thing off! Something was wrong. When I complained to my breast surgeon, she pointed the finger at the radiologist, who pointed the finger at the oncologist. It was an ugly blame game, with me being the loser. I wasn't being heard or helped. Even during maintenance therapy, when I shared how certain medications were making me sick, my old oncologist dismissed me. Thankfully, I found a new oncologist who demonstrated genuine concern and care. This was after I fired my old one. There is nothing wrong with you taking steps to make sure you receive the best care possible by advocating for yourself and choosing the right provider. It was 2020 when I was moved under my new doctor's care, so whenever I saw him, he had a mask on. It took over a year to see the man's whole face, but when I did, we both laughed. Apparently, we met in the early 2000s when I was searching for a physician to deal with Hodgkins. I had had an opportunity to work with him then. It was a full-circle moment that I took as divine confirmation that he was the one I was supposed to work with.

With my previous oncologist, no matter how much I complained about my breast, I was ignored, but with my new one, he said, "Let's do a full work-up even though I don't see or feel anything." That was the kind of care I needed because that full work-up revealed that the cancer had, in fact, returned. In 2021, I was re-diagnosed with breast cancer. I was 48 years old.

For over a year, everyone had been pointing the finger, normalizing my pain because they didn't want to be wrong. I can't imagine what hurdles I would have avoided if someone had just listened to me as soon as I said there was an issue.

Although I was disappointed, this time, with the diagnosis, I wasn't hit as hard emotionally. I knew there was something wrong that whole time, so I was more relieved than anything when it was finally found. My mindset was, "Ok. We're here. Again. Let's knock this thing out." My surgeon prepared to do the mastectomy to remove the breast and then rebuild it using fat from my stomach, which is a process called "The Flap." My ever-eternal optimism was in full throttle about this plan, but it nose-dived when the cancer was discovered to have spread to a few nodules in my lungs. That revelation was a doozy because it meant I was at stage 4 cancer. When the cancer metastasizes, there is no option to do The Flap. All plastic surgery is off the table. As a result, I had to go straight into chemotherapy.

Chemo was rough, and the IVs didn't work. I moved to taking the pills, and finally, the cancer started shrinking. Then I moved to monthly butt injections performed with a huge needle in both butt cheeks. The gel used for these injections needed to be warmed up beforehand. If it wasn't warmed, then the injections would be super painful.

After all of that, I was still experiencing a great deal of pain. Finally, my oncologist and breast surgeon agreed to do a palliative mastectomy on my right side. Afterward, I had radiation. That was another difficult experience because I got burned, and weeks later, it was revealed that my ribs were fractured. That's the thing about radiation; it can take weeks for something like that to surface. Additionally, there emerged a huge hematoma from the surgery that wouldn't drain. That meant that a blood vessel had gotten damaged during surgery and formed a clot. Clearly, treatment for this second round of breast cancer was more brutal than the first. I couldn't have imagined how difficult it would be to recover from all of the added difficulties that would happen. Prior to all of this, I had lowballed my estimation of how much time I would be out of work because I had previously dealt with stage 1A cancer, but this was stage 4. I was using my PTO and short-term disability even before all the surgeries, but eventually, it got to the point where I was no longer able to work every day, and at the end of 2020, we were back in the office. When I would try to work, I was too fatigued and could barely focus. I went out on FMLA, but my job's HR department started hounding me about when I would return. They gave me a deadline that I simply couldn't meet. In this position, I didn't have a lot of job security, but there was nothing I could do about it. I was in the thick of battling for my life. Unfortunately, outside of my good friend that hired me, the company wasn't sympathetic in the least, and for the 2nd time in less than two years, and for the exact same reason, my employer terminated me.

Staci is my daughter and my blessing from God and the most amazing, talented, intelligent and strong person! I have been in awe of her all her life, watching her accomplish so many achievements even while battling cancer, and inspiring women experiences the same traumas. I have so much love and appreciation for her as a woman, mother, daughter, and friend.
- Judi Kirk

"I have worked with PurPose with different events, and she is a dedicated woman who gets the job done, she is very hands-on and strives for the best. I always enjoy a good event with my girl. She is a very strong woman."
~Naré C

CHAPTER 14: BOOB GRIEF

Years ago, I attended a breast cancer fundraising event where a female speaker shared her experience of overcoming breast cancer. "Every patient who has stage 1A breast cancer will eventually experience stage 4 metastatic breast cancer," she announced to the crowd. I was highly upset. How is she going to speak that over us! I was thinking. At the time, I had only experienced stage 1A breast cancer. After my second diagnosis, I knew firsthand that what she said was true. But it still broke my heart to hear it. When you're swimming in a sea of survivors and thrivers, you don't want to hear that you could possibly be taken under by another wave of cancer.

Being re-diagnosed can be discouraging on so many levels. You think you've beaten this monster that has taken others out, only to discover there's another round ahead. Then, when it spreads, your options are limited with plastic surgery, and you have to go through the whole ordeal of treatment all over again. But because when the diagnosis was made, I knew something was wrong, and no one was listening to me, I was more relieved than anything. What really got me in this whole process was losing my breast.

When you lose a breast, you lose a part of yourself. It feels as if you've lost a whole limb of your body. As a woman, your breasts are symbols of attraction. "Come get me!" they're screaming to the world as they jut out of that fancy tight dress or jiggle over that low-cut top. They're what you've innately and subconsciously been trained by culture to use to validate your worth. They're the peak of your femininity, so to speak. They've been with you since puberty and mine even before then since I developed so young. It was a shift for sure to see myself as the attractive vessel that previously harbored double D's. Even now, years later, every once in a while, when I step out of the shower dripping wet, my reflection in the mirror startles me.

In my mind, I think, "*Oh, that's right, my breast is gone.*"

Having a breast removed is a psychological shock on top of all the other changes happening in your body due to the treatment. With loss of any kind comes grief and sometimes shock - again.
In September 2021, when I got fired for the second time, I had a financial burden to add to my list of adjustments. The company I worked for only covered my health insurance for as long as I worked there, so this time around, I didn't have coverage after termination. This hurt on a few levels. Employers have the right to extend FMLA if they'd like to, but in both cases, they chose not to exercise that right. Don't get me wrong, I understand companies are about fulfilling their business needs. However, I believe their treatment of me could have been better. If they really cared about their associates, it would have been.

Immediately after my termination, I applied for social security. Now, why was it that others who I knew applied were able to receive their benefits in a measly couple of months, and my funds didn't get released for nine whole months? For nearly a year, I was scrounging to pay my bills. Though I was able to get some aid for rent, that time period was rough. I don't know about you, but God likes to wake me up in the middle of the night. I have no idea why when He knows I like sleep just as much as the next person. But one night, He got my attention when I woke up in the middle of the night and heard that still small voice. "Give away your group coaching for free," it said. I was surprised, to say the least. I had been praying and praying about provision and stressing on how I was going to make it. Now,

God was telling me to give away something I could have been charging for at a time when I needed money the most. It didn't make sense. But isn't it often that way with God? His thoughts are higher, and when we step out in faith to obey, we see the reward of His instruction. Do you know I offered my group coaching services for free, and within two weeks, I had three new clients paying me a total of $7000?! I had some basic coaching programs that were free on my website, but I had kept the elite program packages that were more advanced available. Folks saw those and bought the elite packages. Those elite programs had been out there, and nobody was paying any attention to them; it was just a matter of timing. I obeyed, and God moved. After dragging my feet, I became a full-fledged entrepreneur. I just needed a little time to get there.

Taking a leap into entrepreneurship is no easy task, especially in my generation when you're taught that the stability and benefits that a 9-to-5 provides are vital to your livelihood.

I was never trained in entrepreneurship and didn't have any models or mentors on this path (other than my middle school teacher), but what I did have was a gift. I was a natural leader and constantly attracted women who were looking for guidance and assistance to manifest their business dreams. I didn't need to obtain a degree to do what I was groomed to do in life. The lessons I had learned in my career were the foundation for what I shared in my coaching programs.

After being fired the second time, I had once again turned my lemons into lemonade. I could have sunk into despair, not seeing how I was going to provide, but keeping my faith and holding on to my tenacity to overcome carried me through another storm. The very thing that set out to take me out, being terminated by my employer, became the incubator for my calling and birthed sustainability in my business. All this while fighting cancer.

I know it seems like a lot, but for most of my journey, I wasn't aware of how unique my numerous physical afflictions were. I knew that others suffered various types of abuse and trauma, so part of my "glass-is-half-full" mentality was built on this view. But even my doctors understood that I was a rare breed, and around the 2nd diagnosis, they brought in a special board to discuss my case. This board included top-notch oncologists who weighed in their thoughts on how to treat me. I was, on all accounts at this point, considered an anomaly, and it would take the best of the best to treat me.

It was after my second round of breast cancer that I got into advocacy. I had been through it so many times, dealing with racist health professionals and the system as a whole. I knew firsthand the great need for minority patients to be heard concerning their health. It was a crying shame that I went nearly a year after my first surgery in pain and pleading for someone to listen. But during that time, instead of doctors listening to me, they made me feel like a nuisance. As if the pain was all in my head.

According to the American Cancer Society, 40% of Black women have a higher mortality rate from breast cancer than white women and a higher mortality rate than any ethnic group in the US. Could this be because our voices aren't being heeded in enough time to prevent the illness from spreading? From killing us? I think so. To assist in leveraging the platform for our struggle, I became a mentor in Cleveland Clinic's Fourth Angel mentorship program. The program is set up so that cancer patients are partnered with someone who has already faced what they're currently facing. Someone with firsthand knowledge. Someone like me. Mentoring has been a great experience for me in finding purpose in all that I've gone through. It encourages me to encourage others, especially on a personal level. I'm the first person in my circle to call when someone receives the diagnosis. I appreciate this role in my community because I'm always at my best when I'm helping someone else.

Outside of being a Fourth Angel, I'm VP of Communications for the Breast Cancer Fund of Ohio, where I handle our annual reporting and other administrative tasks, I am a member of the National Breast Cancer Coalition, and a volunteer and occasional speaker for

Susan G. Komen of Northeast Ohio. At Komen, one of my intentions is to lessen the stigma that major organizations are keeping a cure at bay for breast cancer in order to profit from the disease. I also participate so that their associates have more of an up-close minority presence that will hopefully influence their decision-making concerning the fight against cancer.

Additionally, I participate in Project Lead, an initiative led by The National Breast Cancer Coalition. NBCC is an organization that works with lawmakers, scientists, and survivors/thrivers to end breast cancer. Project Lead equips survivors with scientific knowledge of breast cancer and potential cures to be able to review clinical studies and speak intelligently about it with lawmakers and other government officials. In 2024, I was awarded a scholarship to fly out and participate in their 5-day training course. The funds went towards my flight, other essentials during my stay, and continuing the program.

Wearing all of these hats in the breast cancer-fighting arena is a picture of how all things have worked for my good. The injustices I faced inspired me to align myself with foundations and organizations to gain knowledge to combat these discriminations in the healthcare field.

NaQuari KING Johson

One of my greatest joys has been this little guy. My 'gbaby' is intelligent, loving, and kind. He deserves the world, and I plan to give it to him!

Being around PurPose is inspirational. Not only because she is battling the hardest battle; having cancer, but because she also wears many hats from being a mom to a businesswoman. She made me realize that there is such a thing as willpower.
-JC Smith

CHAPTER 15: SIS, LET ME TAKE MY WIG OFF

Although it was, of course, disappointing, my re-diagnosis didn't really catch me off guard because it was another one of those times where I felt like something was wrong. My breast was still in constant pain, and I had been insisting to my oncologist that something wasn't right. Maybe because I've dealt with cancer too many times, I'm very in tune with my body. But while I was persistently telling my oncologist and surgeon about my pain, they kept dismissing me or pointing the finger at the radiologist. "Oh, well, we just think it's scar tissue," they responded, but they did an ultrasound anyway. Additionally, they did both a CAT scan and breast MRI; both reportedly showed no signs of cancer. Since they were blaming him, I went to my radiologist. Though my radiologist's treatment plan was admittedly the culprit for my ribs being fractured, ultimately, he became my only advocate. And because I wouldn't take no for an answer, he didn't either. He ordered tests STAT as well as a biopsy. The first biopsy result came back negative, but thankfully, my radiologist kept pushing and found a different doctor all the way from Columbus, Ohio, to do another biopsy. That's when it was confirmed. The cancer had returned, and because he kept pressing and wouldn't let it go, we found it. By then, the cancer was bigger, as shown in the ultrasound.

Finally, I was being heard, but it took too much effort for it to happen. This was my third diagnosis of breast cancer and my sixth time dealing with cancer in general. I was 51 years old.

Let me just say that the second biopsy was very uncomfortable, to say the least. They took a total of 10 samples. In the previous biopsy, I was under twilight, but with this one, there was no twilight, just lots of numbing. But the numbing didn't remove the immense pressure being exerted on an area that was already painful. As patients, we are our first physicians. We know our bodies. I can't reiterate this enough. If those who are in a position to help are not adhering to your voice, seek another health professional. Cancer is a life-or-death issue and can't afford to be taken lightly.

Later on, my surgeon shared that when she did my surgery after the second diagnosis, she did see malignancy on the muscle behind the breast. And guess what? That's exactly where the cancer was found this third time. That meant that either she didn't get it or she didn't At the time of my re-diagnosis, I was keeping my plate full, just how I liked it. I was truly living on purpose. My love life was thriving, too, and by then, I was engaged. I was even gearing up for a trip to Cancun with friends, but the news of this re-diagnosis halted everything. My position as Project Lead was put on the back burner, although thankfully, my scholarship was transferred to the following year for me to participate. But because I'm such a go-getter, it was still a letdown that I had to forgo all of my plans.

There were some changes happening in my home at the time that weren't so great either. My mother had been officially diagnosed with Dementia and moved in so that I could be her primary caretaker. That dynamic was a difficult one to have in the midst of my need to care for myself. Because of her mental state, she didn't understand I had cancer and wasn't able to assist and support me with what I was going through. This stirred up my awareness of our relationship. My mother loves me, yet the way we have always functioned is me taking on a parental role with her. A great example of this was when I was first diagnosed with Hodgkins and learned that the side effect of chemotherapy was death. I ended up being the comforter to her and my ex in that situation when I should have been the one being comforted. In this season, I realized that I was and have always been "the mom."

My mom wasn't the only one who depended on me when I was in need. On the heels of my re-diagnosis, I was bombarded with needy people asking for help. Even while receiving treatment in the hospital, folks were reaching out to me to perform services for them. I have always been a giver and, as a result, have naturally attracted takers. It was nuts. I know I'm a strong person and don't walk around like a victim, but it's mind-blowing sometimes to see how selfish some people can be. Just because I don't choose to walk around sad doesn't mean I'm not sick!

It is at the time of writing this book that I'm in the throes of this third diagnosis of breast cancer and sixth diagnosis of cancer. I've been dealing with some form of cancer most of my life, since the tender age of 14 when I had those lumps under my armpits from Follicular Lymphoma. Every decade of my life has been scarred by cancer, yet somehow, I've managed to still accomplish more than others who haven't had this ongoing life challenge. I don't say that to toot my own horn. Instead, I say it is a statement of encouragement. If I can do it, you can do it too.

I believe we can learn from every trial in life. As draining and painful as battling another round of cancer has been on my body, I can at least say that my mental health is getting better due to implementing better boundaries. Just as I've awakened to the unhealthy way that I and my mother have functioned, I've awakened to how I've functioned in unhealthy ways with others. There's a reason folks will hit me up while I'm in the hospital bed to do x, y, and z for them. They know I will do it. But this time around, I don't have it to give. When I received this last diagnosis, I knew I needed to tend to my self-care and amped up my boundaries when it came to doing what was best for me. I couldn't keep being there for everyone else, and I wasn't even there for myself.
I learned to ignore my needs at a young age. Growing up with the parents I had, under the abuse I suffered, made being others oriented

and self-reliant protective mechanisms that helped me to survive. But at 51, I can't afford to minimize my needs any longer. This third round of breast cancer has taught me that. Previously, I would wheel my whole hospital bed to an event! Now, I have no problem delegating to someone else to take my place if I'm not feeling well. Now I have quality people in my life who I not only feed into, but they can feed into me too. One tool in healing my self-view and values I used is taking Reiki. In one of my sessions, I learned that one of the words related to "breast" is "unworthy." That was a surprise. I had never felt I was unworthy, but I realized I was willing to give up my peace to help someone else. That means I was willing to help someone else, even to my own detriment. There must be some part of me that felt unworthy! In my coaching and various leadership positions, I've taught about worth and value but unknowingly didn't implement that teaching in my own life. My mindset was outward-focused, and I wasn't sitting with myself and looking inward. It's understandable, given the level of trauma I've faced throughout my entire life, but it's clear that my repetitive affliction from cancer is not just a physical assault. It's related to my mental, emotional, spiritual, and psychological health as well. I am tackling this thing differently this time, and as a result, I know I'll see the victory. Again.

Because I'm facing what is called a local recurrence, which is when cancer reappears in the same place, the plastic surgeon stated that surgery was going to be several hours with a 6-8 day hospital stay afterward. This is considered a radical surgery and very labor intensive. It was decided that I would do chemo first to shrink the size of the tumor some before surgery. To date, I have one more cycle of treatment left and then six weeks before surgery. My last scan showed NO shrinkage at all. The tumor is the same size. Additionally, the chemotherapy I'm being treated with is Sacituzumab Govitecan-Hziy, and I have not tolerated it well. It actually landed me in the hospital, causing me to lose over 23 pounds! I'm also preparing to get prosthetic ribs to replace the ones that were fractured. The surgeons need to rebuild my chest wall with The Flap from my stomach, and I may have to resume chemo after surgery. So, it's been a rocky road, to say the least, but given my story, how could I expect anything less?

Out of all of the trauma, pain, and surgeries I've faced, though, one of the things that has irked me along the way is wearing wigs. It wasn't necessarily the hair loss that got me with chemo, but the weighty, itchy, uncomfortable wig I would throw on for my outings. When I get home from an event that inspired me to rock one, as soon as I hit the door, I'm ripping it off. That is when I am most authentic. When the thing that is weighing me down is removed. At my core, I just want to sit with my sisters, chop it up, have some laughs, and take my wig off. Taking off my wig is symbolic of me being unapologetically, and I'm glad to say that has happened to a higher degree with this last diagnosis. I'm no longer people-pleasing and putting others before me. I am making my health the priority it needs to be and will no longer sacrifice it for the sake of someone else. I am taking off my wig.

These days, I'm focusing on treatment and recovery and still plan to do everything I've been called to. The timing may not be what I expected when executing some of these projects, but I'm certain they will all get done when they're supposed to.

In 2025 I'll be married and will resume all of my leadership responsibilities. I'm a firm believer we were created for purpose and my purpose isn't finished yet. Not even a little bit.

When I started this book, I had no idea I would be re-diagnosed. Surely, I had been through *enough* before this last diagnosis to inspire *somebody* with my story! But that is where my faith comes in, I know without a doubt that no matter what comes, no matter how many challenges surface, I am victorious. And because I am victorious, I believe wholeheartedly that, sis, you are too!

Writing "Hold on Sis, Let Me Take My Wig Off" with Staci was truly an honor. Not many have endured the levels of insurmountable challenges she's faced in so many different areas of her life. I can't imagine having endured the breadth of hardships she has and still maintain a positive outlook. Staci has an admirable ability to encourage others while navigating the waves of brutal circumstances. This writing project was a beautiful eye-opening experience for us both and I'm blessed to be chosen to partner in sharing this powerful account of her resilience and multiple triumphs over cancer.

-Nicole D. Miller

A Note from the Author

Hey Friend Heyyyyy!

This book was a labor of love—one that took me on a journey I wasn't entirely prepared for. Not because I had to revisit the traumas I've faced in my life, but because I didn't fully realize how all the pieces fit together until I started writing. I thought I was doing this to love on you, to show you how to overcome adversity and rise stronger. But somewhere along the way, it became a love letter to myself as well.

I've spent most of my life giving—sometimes so much that I lost track of who I was. I didn't realize just how much I had gone through; how much I had given away to people who didn't deserve me. But now, looking back, I know that the decision to write this book was all God. He gave me the courage to confront parts of myself I had buried just to survive. And I give Him all the glory and honor, because without His grace, the gifts that are my children, and the love of my life, I wouldn't have made it. Marvin Sapp sang it best, "I never would have made it."

But this book isn't just about me—it's for you, too. Whether you're overcoming something right now, still healing from the past, or bracing yourself for an unexpected storm, I want you to know that you are built to survive. Not just survive but thrive. Throughout this process, I prayed for you. I prayed that Nicole and I would write the words your heart needed to hear and that God would speak to you through these pages. I will keep praying for you if you promise to pray for me, too.

By the time you read this, I will have fought and beaten cancer for the sixth time. And let me tell you, this last round was something else. It was tough but knowing that my family and friends were waiting for me (that includes you now), kept me going.

I love you, and I surely love myself too!

With all my heart and without my wig (lol),
~Staci PurPose Kirk

Dedication

Yes, the back of the book is where I thought you would find the most significance and honor. Why? Because you had to read and experience what I've been through to understand the importance of your presence in my life (although I have a feeling you already know). When I think of you and our journey together, the word INFINITY comes to mind. There just is no me without you.

Together we've beat all the odds and gone against every opposition with fierceness and grace. While writing this book, I realized how much you've needed me and I you – and now here we are.

Many may read this dedication, and it resonate with them as it mirrors the relationship they have with me, and many may wonder who exactly *you* are… but I know you know and that's all that matters.

I will always love you, hold space for you, and have gratitude for who you are and will forever be, for me.

www.ingramcontent.com/pod-product-compliance
Lightning Source LLC
Chambersburg PA
CBHW041722070526
44585CB00001B/10